South Bend to Spring Valley

The Davids-Sims Story

By

Eric and Joyce Christianson

Published by Hemingway Publishers

Cover design by Hemingway Publishers

ISBN: Printed in the United States

Dedication

This book is dedicated to my loving wife of 44 years, Joyce Davids Christianson. She passed away on January 1, 2023, at the way-too-young age of 66. Joyce was the love of my life and my reason for being. Her passing has left a hole in my heart that will never completely mend. I carry on only because I must. The driving force behind such sentiment is simply to live a life that would make her proud... and to complete a task she began, which was of great importance to her.

Joyce was but a year old when she and her parents moved to a farm in southeastern Minnesota. It was two years thereafter that events would unfold which would leave a lasting impression on Joyce. Her mother, Roselyn, was a God-fearing woman, someone who would not stand idly by when faced with an unjust situation she could remedy. That attitude... that sense of morality (which Joyce inherited)... resulted in an intervention that would forever alter the lives of her kin, and those of the Sims, a black family from South Bend, Indiana.

The entire experience garnered national attention and significantly impacted Joyce, so much so that she desired to someday write a book about it, as her mother kept a scrapbook of letters and related news articles. Though many aspire to be a published author, the nuts and bolts of writing a book can be overwhelming, so much so as to stunt the most important part – getting started.

As an adult, Joyce's life was filled with other things she was passionate about: music, animals (she was a vegetarian), and family activities, just to name a few. Hence, writing the book was pushed to the back burner. It wasn't until her health began to fail that a sense of urgency emerged to embark on this arduous odyssey. Joyce's goal was to chronicle the adventure via the correspondence between her mother and Mr. Sims. Hence, the first step was to transcribe the hand-written letters (in cursive and faded over time) into a file on our desktop. Sadly, health issues continued to mount, zapping her energy and motivation. She asked me to assist in this endeavor so, of course, I obliged. With the typing of the letters complete, it became obvious that more would be required of me to make Joyce's dream a reality, as her kidneys were failing and dialysis was not an option. We opted for hospice care, and as she lay in the hospital bed set up for her in our living room, life draining from her body, she asked but one thing of me: "Eric, finish the book."

South Bend to Spring Valley: the Davids-Sims Story is a tale of phenomenal friendship, one that overcame numerous hardships and blossomed into something so beautiful... so impactful that my wife's dying wish was for me to tell the story. So, I did, not for fame or fortune, but to leave a legacy for one of God's greatest creations, one that implores Americans of all creeds and colors to set aside their differences and come together for the good of humanity. What the Sims and Davids accomplished in an era known for its racial strife is remarkable. They truly did judge people by the content of their character, not the color of their skin. Martin Luther King, Jr. would be proud... and so was Joyce.

Table of Contents

Chapter 1: How it All Started

"It was the best of times, it was the worst of times." [1] No, this is not an adaptation of *A Tale of Two Cities*. I merely borrowed a line from Charles Dickens that aptly sums up a tumultuous time in our nation's history known simply as the '60s. This turbulent decade is infamous for not one or two but multiple political assassinations, not to mention the debacle known as the Vietnam War, as well as the intensifying of the Civil Rights Movement. Racial tension was at an all-time high, fueling unrest, protests, and riots. This evocative canvas provided the backdrop for an unlikely chain of events, which would bring worldwide attention to race relations in the United States and forever alter the course of two families: one black (the Sims) and one white (the Davids).

Marienus and Roselyn Davids lived on a small farm near Spring Valley, Minnesota, with their two young children, Joyce and Gregory. They earned a modest income living off the land, which included growing oats, corn, and soybeans. Meat, milk, and eggs were provided via the family's livestock and poultry. Their lifestyle was simple, and their work ethic strong, as was their Christian faith, which sustained them during difficult times. While Marienus tended the land and animals, Roselyn cooked, canned, and taught piano lessons to supplement the family's income. Those who knew them would tell you that Roselyn was the most godly woman they knew and Marienus

---

[1] Dickens, Charles, 1812-1870. 1961. A Tale of Two Cities. New York, Macmillan.

- Sharkey as he was known to his friends (after Jack Sharkey, the iconic boxer) - the most gentle and humble of men.

Our story actually begins in the previous decade – June of 1959, to be more precise. One of Roselyn's favorite pastimes was listening to the radio, specifically to programs she found informative and/or inspirational. One such program was *Image Series*. This NBC-sponsored foray into current events and issues featured as host the prominent writer and columnist Bob Considine.

As part of a sub-series, *Image: Minorities*, the topic one evening was the plight of Black families in urban America. His guest was a Mr. David Sims. He, his wife, Ruby, and (at the time) eight children lived in South Bend, Indiana. David lamented that he could not find and keep steady employment, thanks to the politics and economics of the times. They lived off a scant weekly unemployment check, which wasn't enough even to put adequate food on the table, let alone pay the rent and other expenses. What really perked up Roselyn's ears was a comment made by Mr. Sims that he had never been invited into a white person's home as a guest. Roselyn was the kind of person who would right every wrong, were it within her power to do so. While other folks might have simply been aghast by the comment, Roselyn was spurred to take action. She turned to her husband (who had recently come into the house from milking cows and joined her at the dining room table) with a twinkle in her eye that Marienus had come to know all too well and the two began discussing the ramifications of inviting to their rural Minnesota home an African American family of ten they had never met, some 446 miles away.

Having agreed upon this course of action, Roselyn got in touch with the local radio station (KROC out of Rochester) that aired the program. Her request to get contact information on the Sims was denied, standard operating procedure for a radio station, especially given the circumstances. It was eventually agreed upon that she could write the Sims, informing them of her offer. The station would forward the letter to NBC Studios in New York. With any luck, it would reach the producer of the Image Series program, the legendary Peter Lassally, who would then, hopefully, forward her correspondence to Mr. Sims. For that, a courier would be needed. Enter one Dennis Dowdell of the South Bend Urban League. Considine had utilized Dowdell to secure someone who could adequately portray the sad state of affairs for most Black families trying to make ends meet in White America. Mr. Sims was that someone.

Despite the preponderance of potential pitfalls, the letter did arrive at its final destination, a testament to the diligence of everyone involved. Upon receipt of the magnanimous missive, Mr. Sims was floored that any white family would make such an offer, and he certainly did not suffer from a lack of opinions on how to handle the matter. Many friends and family were skeptical of the proposition and advised that he turn it down, lest it be a ruse to lynch them. Despite this, Mr. Sims did put pen to paper, thanking the Davids for their offer, but declining, as he had recently gone back to work and could not afford the trip, as this job provided the family's sole source of income.

This, as they say, was the beginning of a beautiful friendship, as Roselyn and David would go on to write to each other's families regularly. David would regale his newfound friends with tales of his children's escapades, though his correspondence often turned dark as he railed against discrimination and racism. Roselyn would impart stories of life on the farm, going so far as to ask the Sims children to name a recently born calf (which they did – Rapanza). She even persuaded her church to take up a collection to pay for the Sims' expenses if they could carve out a window of time to come for a visit. This act of kindness moved the Sims beyond words, cementing their belief that the intentions of this white family from small-town Minnesota were indeed pure.

Both families kept Lassally and Considine in the loop as to the progress of their budding bi-racial relationship. The two titans were so impressed with the developments that Considine requested permission to use their correspondence to develop a story he hoped to feature in one of his columns for the New York Journal American.

The Davids and Sims became as close as families could be without meeting in person, having only corresponded by mail. But would the Sims finally make that journey from South Bend to Spring Valley? Did the Sims reciprocate and host the Davids at their home?

The rest of the story is told in their own words as what follows is the aforementioned correspondence between Roselyn Davids and David Sims. Most of the letters, hand-written and faded over time, were too illegible to be scanned, but copies of many of the original typed letters were included. This correspondence is supplemented with content found in articles from local, state, and even national publications, much of which was derived from interviews with reporters. Roselyn kept a scrapbook of such things, but, of course, not every publisher permitted the use of its article's content. Those that did are cited and given their due. Though few in number, first-hand accounts from surviving friends and family members are also incorporated so that the reader may gain insight from those who directly experienced this momentous melding of Black and White.

Sadly, given the times, not everyone was supportive of such an endeavor. Both families received much hate mail on the subject, some of which is included, so that the reader may gain perspective regarding what the Sims and Davids had to deal with in overcoming obstacles to forge a race-transcending fellowship, one that would gain them world-renown (though neither family sought it) and enrich these two valiant families - and those who knew them - beyond what they ever could have imagined.

Chapter 2: A Friendship Born

Gentlemen:

If your program on minority groups is appreciated by others the way it is by us, I suppose this letter will be one among thousands sending their thanks for the research and time that you have spent making it possible. We think these things should be said.

Last night my husband and I were listening to the program about the Negroes on KROC Rochester, Minn. When David Sims told about his situation and at the end of the interview said he had never had a visit to a white person's home, we suddenly realized that here is something we can do personally about it.

We love company, and we love to visit folks. We wonder if there is any way that this family could spend a week with us sometime in August. We say August because there is about a two-week period there when the oats are harvested, and the beans and corn are not ready to harvest yet, and it would give us time to really entertain them and get acquainted. Also, we would be having good things like sweet corn and vegetables ready in the garden.

Perhaps they should know something about us so they will know this is a genuine offer of friendship we send them.

My husband is Marienus Davids, age 41. I am Mary Roselyn Davids, age 29. We have 2 little children. Joyce Eileen will be 3 in August. Gregory Michael will be 1 in August. The children have 2 puppies, Tupper and April.

We are Christians and are members of the Sumner Center Evangelical United Brethren Church, where my husband is a trustee, and I belong to the Woman's Missionary Society and direct the church choir.

Our home is modest but very comfortable and is truly open as a place to make a practical application of Christian Social Relations.

The only problem that we see now is that of getting them here (transportation). If you know, or they know, any way of getting them here, then please give them our cordial invitation to spend a week with us this August.

Our best regards.

Sincerely,

Mary Roselyn Davids (Mrs. Marienus)

~~~~~~

And there you have it – the letter that started it all. Keep in mind that this was written in 1959 (precise date unknown). It has not been edited in any way to make it politically correct. The term "Negro" was commonly used at that time, and no malice was intended by said usage. Also note that the letter was not addressed directly to the Sims family, as the Davids were not permitted access to the Sims' address in South Bend, Indiana.

The letter was initially sent to KROC in Rochester, MN, the radio station that aired the program. It was then forwarded to the *Image Series* radio program at the radio division of NBC. It made its way into the hands of Peter Lassally, the program's producer.

What follows are letters Mr. Lassally sent to Mr. Dowdell and to the Davids family.

August 20, 1959

Mr. Dennis Dowdell
South Bend Urban League
724 Western Avenue
South Bend, Indiana

Dear Mr. Dowdell:

Enclosed you will find a letter we received from a couple in Minnesota in response to our "Image: Minorities" program on the Negro in America. They are very graciously offering their home to Mr. David Simms for a visit.

I would appreciate it if you would pass this letter on to Mr. Simms. Please let us know the results.

Thanking you in advance for your continued help.

Very truly yours,

Peter Lassally
Producer Image Series

PL/nl

Enclosures: 1

NATIONAL BROADCASTING COMPANY, INC.

A SERVICE OF RADIO CORPORATION OF AMERICA

RCA Building, Radio City, New York 20, N.Y.

CIRCLE 7-8300

August 20, 1959

Mr. and Mrs. Marienus Davids
Box 100   R.R. #3
Spring Valley, Minn.

Dear Mr. and Mrs. Davids:

I am sorry for the delay in answering your letter.

We have forwarded your letter to Mr. Dennis Dowdell of
the South Bend, Indiana, Urban League. Mr. Dowdell was
our South Bend contact who found Mr. David Simms for us
to interview. I am sure Mr. Dowdell will pass your
letter on to Mr. Simms and you should be hearing an
answer to your kind invitation some time in the near
future.

Thank you for your interest in our programs. Yours
is the type of response we like to receive. Please
let us know the results after you hear from Mr. Simms.

Very truly yours,

Peter Lassally
Producer Image Series

PL/nl

Readers unfamiliar with Peter Lassally may not understand the magnitude of this event. Lassally started his career in radio and TV as a page for NBC. He eventually worked his way up to being a producer, not just for the *Image Series* but for more well-known programs like Arthur Godfrey's television show. His major claim to fame came years later when he took over as executive producer for *The Tonight Show* in 1970. After Johnny Carson retired in 1992, Lassally went on to become the executive producer of *Late Night with David Letterman*. He was also executive producer of *The Late Late Show with Tom Snyder* from 1995 to 1999 and even mentored Jon Stewart when he guest-hosted for Snyder. Lassally certainly earned his nickname: "the host whisperer."[2]

So... had KROC not agreed to dispatch that first letter from Mrs. Davids to NBC... had it not reached Mr. Lassally... had he not forwarded it to Mr. Dowdell... none of this would ever have come to pass.

But it did. And thanks to the aforementioned trio of fine gentlemen associated with the Image Series radio program, as well as the South Bend Urban League, the letter finally reached its intended destination. Oh, to be a fly on the wall as David Sims opened and read a letter (to himself at first and later out loud to his wife and children) from a white family he did not know extending an invitation to him and his ménage of ten to come to rural Minnesota for a week for no other

---

[2] Peter Lassally. (2024, April 30). In Wikipedia. https://en.wikipedia.org/wiki/Peter_Lassally

reason than the opportunity to visit and get to know one another. What follows is the response Mr. Sims penned, no doubt, after much prayer and consideration, especially given the enormity of the undertaking. He likely faced skepticism from non-immediate family members who were concerned that Roselyn's motives might not be altruistic. After all, what white folk invite Black folk they don't know into their home for tea and crumpets? There had to be an angle, perhaps a nefarious one. Yet, despite all this, and with the support of his wife and children, Mr. Sims chose to believe in Roselyn's sincerity, as reflected in the tone and verbiage of his reply.

~~~~~~

314 S. Illinois Street
South Bend, Indiana
August 27, 1959

Dear Mr. & Mrs. Davids:

We received your wonderful letter only today. Words cannot describe our heartfelt thanks and appreciation for the invitation extended by you and your family to our family. Our only regret is that we cannot accept your hospitality at this particular time. To avoid lengthy details, the corporation where I am employed was closed down for approximately a month for model change. I've just recently returned to work, and my work is my only source of income. With a total of ten in family, I'm sure you understand why we cannot accept your invitation at this time. However, if in the future, the invitation remains open and we are financially able, we would be more than glad to accept. We are so sorry we did not receive your letter so we could have answered sooner.

It certainly makes us feel good to know that we have allies in the struggle and fight for freedom. It's good religious people like you that help restore a person's faith in humanity, and we appreciate your attitude and stand when you say you also appreciate the program "Image Minorities." We have something in common. We feel more of this sort of programming is needed all over our country, not only on radio but also on T.V. Then people would be able to understand that our aim and purposes in life are the same as theirs, to live a full, happy and cultivating life during our short life span. We are also religious people of protestant faith. We are members of New Salem Baptist Church and are in the process of building now. My wife and four of our children participate in the church choir. Two months ago, they organized a family choral group and were invited to sing at several local churches.

When we told the children of your wonderful invitation to us, they were so happy they wanted to leave right away.

Our family consists of 10 people. Listed in order, I will start with myself.

David Sims – age 31, my wife Ruby Sims – age 31; daughters Charlotte – age 11 and Carla Diane – age 10; sons David Sims III – age 14, Harold Sims

```
- age 12, and Paul - age 8; daughters Cheryl - age
6 and Fredonya - age 5, and son Lee Charles Sims -
age 2. We sincerely would appreciate hearing from
you at your earliest convenience.

Sincerely yours,
Mr. & Mrs. David Sims and Family
```

To further expound upon the information in that letter, David and Ruby lived in a modest house in South Bend, Indiana, with their eight – eventually to be nine – children. The employment David spoke of was with Studebaker Corp. He will speak more on that topic in subsequent letters. Despite the hesitancy of some to trust the motives of this unfamiliar white family, David and Ruby's children were not among them. As stated in the letter, they were so excited about this new adventure that they wanted to leave right away, lending credence to the notion that racism is far more nurture than nature.

But alas, their finances would not allow it, so such a visit would have to wait for another time. All the better, as it turned out, as it gave David and Roselyn more time to correspond by mail so that the families could get to know each other better. And correspond they did, several more times over the next couple of years, going into much greater detail about each and every member of both families, as well as things like favorite pastimes, hobbies, accomplishments, and, of course, the politics of the time.

The patriarch of the Sims household witnessed and suffered first-hand the difficulties of growing up Black in a White America. The economy at the time was poor, and jobs were hard to come by and harder still to keep, especially for someone of his color. Such experiences would sully a lesser man, but he did not let such hardships neuter his faith in God, and he truly believed that people of all races could and would eventually come together so that all Americans could live in harmony. Mr. Sims' strong Christian beliefs are discernible in his opening correspondence with the Davids family but really shine through in subsequent letters, much to the delight of Roselyn and Marienus.

~~~~~~

Sept. 15, 1959

Dear Mr. & Mrs. Sims & Children,

First of all, let me tell you how happy we were when we got your letter of August 27th.

We are so sorry that you won't be able to visit us as soon as we had hoped you could, but please be sure that you are so welcome whenever you can get here.

Perhaps you could plan to come during next year's model change, but until then, we would be so happy to keep getting a little more acquainted by mail.

We are writing you this letter from Branson, Missouri, where we are staying in a little cabin – high in the Ozark Mountains by Lake Taneycomo. My grandmother will be 80 next March and still is able to do some traveling, but she needs someone to drive for her so my husband and I and my mother are doing it for her, and of course, we enjoy the trip, also.

We will arrive home on September 26th.

I showed our pastor, Rev. Utzman, the letter you wrote us and he was happy about it. He suggested that when you come, we would all enjoy some of your music at our church, too.

Does any of your family play the piano? We have a little old-fashioned pump organ, and it is tuned to go with the piano, so when we find someone who plays, we have some real good times playing duets and singing.

My husband and I have an especially warm spot in our hearts for you Baptist folks because when I was going to Iowa State Teachers College, the folks at the Baptist Student Center there were very good to me. Then, when we were married, the wedding was at the Student Center, and the minister was a very dear lady Baptist minister.

We will be so happy when we can actually visit with you but until then, we shall eagerly be awaiting your letters. We were so happy the children wanted to come. We think we owe NBC a great debt for helping us find some more new friends.

Love,
Mr. & Mrs. M. Davids and family

314 S. Illinois Street
South Bend, Indiana
November 12, 1959

Dear Mr. and Mrs. Davids & Children,

We received your letter dated Sept. 15 with profound eagerness and great joy. Like yourself, we feel indebted to NBC for aiding us in finding friends like you.

With the realization that we should have answered your letter sooner, we decided to wait until this date so the children's school photos could be included in the reply. This way, you can get a sort of bird's eye view of some parts of what the Sims family consists of. In our next letter, we will try to include a snapshot of the baby, Ruby, my wife, and myself. We would appreciate an exchange of photos as a further step in getting acquainted.

We were happy to hear of the wonderful vacation the family was able to enjoy in the Ozarks. We were confident it was refreshing, exciting, and afforded all of you memories that you can treasure for a lifetime. It's also gratifying to know the long life span enjoyed by your grandmother. To be active at that age is really something to be appreciated by everyone. Presently, no member of our family plays any musical instrument. Charlotte, our oldest daughter, expressed her desire to do so; however, with a limited income and a family our size, it has been impossible for us to afford. We told the children of your pastor's offer to sing in the church. They said they would consider it an honor and be extremely proud to accept the engagement when and if we get there.

Our family shall work hard and look forward to the many months ahead until next Aug. I hope we can make it. We want you to know the friendship shown in your letters is certainly heart-warming and welcomed by all of us. In all sincerity, we certainly live in hope that this friendship can and will develop into a never-ending bond of man's faith in and understanding of his fellow man as our belief was intended at the beginning of man's creation.

In closing, everyone sends their best regards in hoping you all have a wonderful Thanksgiving. We expect and desire to hear from you at your earliest convenient time.

Sincerely,
Mr. & Mrs. David Sims & Family

The aforementioned photos from the previous Sims letter appear here.

Harold Sims

David Sims III

Charlotte Sims

Carla Sims

Paul Sims

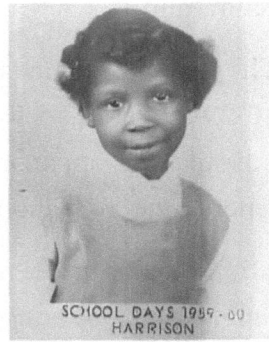

Cheryl Sims

Fredonya Sims

19

Chapter 3: The Proposal

Both families appeared to be getting along famously at this point and are very grateful to NBC for making their long-distance friendship possible, something that Mrs. Davids felt Peter Lassally should know about, especially since she promised to keep him in the loop about how things were progressing between the two households.

What follows are seven letters, each setting in motion events that would eventually lead to the worldwide notoriety of the Sims-Davids fellowship.

The first was composed and sent to Mr. Lassally by Mrs. Davids on 10-29-59 (prior to receiving the previous letter from David Sims). Lassally was apparently so moved by its contents that he fired off a letter to the Sims, hoping to capitalize on this goodwill.

Mr. Sims, in turn, wrote back to Lassally, explaining that he and his family would be happy to promote their newfound friendship with the Davids if it resulted in the enhancement of race relations, but only if Roselyn and family also agreed to the use of their correspondence by Bob Considine as outlined in the letter. He included a copy of this response with the letter he sent to Mr. and Mrs. Davids, informing them of Considine's intentions.

The fifth letter is a response back to Mr. Sims from the Davids in which they express their feelings on the matter, of course, but also have some wonderful farm news. Following that is an apology to Mrs. Davids from Mr. Sims regarding the confusion surrounding the Considine proposal, as well as a response to the calf conundrum.

The final missive is from Lassally, who implores Dowdell to furnish that first missing letter (later discovered) so that Considine may proceed.

~~~~~~

R.R.#3 Box 100
Spring Valley, Minn.
October 29, 1959

Mr. Peter Lassally Producer Image Series

Dear Mr. Lassally:

In the letter that you sent us dated August 20, 1959 you requested that we let you know the results of our invitation to Mr. & Mrs. David Sims and their family to be our house guests.

Perhaps the best way to answer you is to send you the letter they sent us upon receiving our invitation. As you will see when you read it, it is financially impossible just now for them to come.

However, we assured them that our invitation is always open and I'm trying to think of some way to earn some money to help bring them here.

We are so concerned for them now, that maybe the steel strike will put him out of work and they will have all they can do to make ends meet at home. Somehow though, we hope to find a way to bring the family here, and we shall be glad to let you know how we are coming with our project.

We feel we certainly owe you at NBC a great debt for making this contact for us. Thank you.

Sincerely,
Mr. & Mrs. Marienus Davids

NATIONAL BROADCASTING COMPANY, INC.

A SERVICE OF RADIO CORPORATION OF AMERICA

RCA Building, Radio City, New York 20, N.Y.

CIRCLE 7-8300

November 12, 1959

Mr. and Mrs. David Sims
314 S. Illinois Street
South Bend, Indiana

Dear Mr. and Mrs. Sims:

This is in reference to the invitation you and your family have
received from Mr. and Mrs. Davids of Spring Valley, Minnesota, to
visit with them in their home. By our request, the Davids family
have kept us informed as to the outcome of their invitation, and
we are happy to hear that you and your family are planning to visit
with them as soon as it is financially possible.

Mr. Bob Considine, narrator of the "Image: Minorities" series on
which you appeared, is very anxious to use your new-found friendship with the Davids family as the subject for one of his columns
in the New York Journal American. In order to do so, he would
like to see all the letters which you have received from the Davids
family, including the first letter. If, by some chance, you have
saved them, would you please send them to me at the above address,
and I will send them on to Mr. Considine? We will photostat them
and send them back to you as soon as possible.

We of the "Image" department have been very gratified by this
result of your appearance on our program, and are very anxious to
be kept informed of the future relationship of your two families.
Please let us hear from you as soon as possible.

Very truly yours,

Peter Lassally
Producer Image Series

PL/nl

23

Eric and Joyce Christianson

314 S. Illinois Street
South Bend, Indiana
November 18, 1959

Mr. Peter Lassally
Producer Image Series
National Broadcasting Co. Inc.
RCA Bldg. 30 Rockefeller Plaza
New York, 20, New York

Dear Mr. Lassally:

I appreciate your offer to use my correspondence
with the Davids family in Mr. Considine's column. However,
I feel that I would like to have the Davids consent and
approval before forwarding letters to you.

I would also like to take this opportunity to
express our appreciation for our appearance on the Image
Series. We feel that this is timely and welcome to all
people, and should continue.

As soon as I have a reply from the Davids family,
I will correspond with you.

Sincerely,

David Sims

314 S. Illinois St
South Bend, Indiana
November 18, 1959

Dear Mr. & Mrs. Davids:

     Enclosed is a letter received by me from the
National Broadcasting Station requesting that our correspondence
exchange be used by Mr. Bob Considine in his column. We, however,
felt that we must have your consent or approval before releasing
these letters. Naturally, if the exchange of correspondence
furthers the gains in the field of race relations, we would be
overjoyed to be a part of it. Also I am enclosing a copy of
my reply to N. B. C. so you will know our feeling and I would
appreciate hearing from you as soon as possible, as the N.B.C.
studio is awaiting my reply.

                         Sincerely

                         David Sims

November 23, 1959

Dear Mr. & Mrs. Sims,

Your letter arrived here Friday, and we are simply delighted to have the pictures of your lovely family. You folks are certainly to be congratulated for their bright, happy faces. They look like very happy children. We dearly love children and feel they are God's richest gift to us.

Now, as to Bob Considine using our letters. We have considered the matter very carefully this weekend. We are a little shy about it, as we would be distressed if anything should come between us forming a normal, friendly relationship with you folks. We talked with our pastor about it, though, and he feels, too, that these steps on building Christian social relations should be brought to the attention of the public. There is so much tragedy in the news along this line. So, if there is something to be gained in the field of race relations in the publication of these letters then we are duty bound to let them be used. It will be alright with us.

We want to thank you very much for considering us before sending the letters on to Mr. Considine. It was very thoughtful of you.

Our little girl is also enjoying the children's pictures. She studies them and wants to go over them again and again, always having us give her each child's correct name. We are wondering if she will be able to greet the children by name when they meet.

We are busy picking corn. Marienus and a neighbor are working together on it. It has been quite cold this fall, so we will be thankful to have it done soon. Then old man winter can do all it likes. We shall be ready for him.

Joyce was out with her dad the other evening doing the milking and came running back to the house to report that Mardelle, the little Guernsey cow, had a new baby calf. It's a little girl calf, and we wondered if your children would like to name her. We won't give it a name until we hear from them.

We are hoping to spend Thanksgiving with Marienus' family and Christmas with Roselyn's people.

It would be hard to make a complete list of all our blessings, but if a list were made, our growing friendship with you folks would certainly be on it.

As always,
Marienus & Roselyn Davids, Joyce, and Gregory

314 So. Ill. St.
So. Bend, Ind.
Dec. 3, 1959

Mr. & Mrs. Davids & Children,

Dear friends, we received your letter of Nov. 23, and, as always, we were exceedingly glad to hear from you folks again. The pictures of your youngsters won over our hearts. They seem to be the picture of health and spirit; that is something to be thankful for. Our youngest daughter, Fredonya, immediately remarked, "Look, Mother, that little girl is standing on the chair with her shoes on," referring to Joyce. It was quite amusing to us. She forgot that when she was Joyce's age, her action was identical.

I'm afraid that we got the wrong impression from Mr. Lassally's letter when he stated that, by request, you folks had kept him informed, etc. We assumed that he meant that a similar request had been made of you folks.

That is why we spoke of the letter exchange in our permission letter to you. We didn't realize our mistake until we received your letter. We hope NBC understands that. After talking with our minister, the Rev. F. W. Johnson, we forwarded your letter to NBC with a request that they give us a little advance knowledge as to how Mr. Considine intends to bring our friendship to the attention of the public. Ruby and I were thinking the other day why

NBC requested and solicited to use your letter out of the thousands they must have received. We came to the conclusion none could have been more impressive than yours as to sincerity. We feel it must have won the hearts of the people in the studio as it did ours. Somehow, people can feel sincerity and pureness of heart, even though they haven't experienced personal contact with the people. You folks and your minister, the Rev. Utzman, impress us as being worthy of the Christian principle you represent. And heaven knows we're proud to be acquainted and associated with your friendship. We feel that Christians such as yourselves are the only people capable of providing the kind of leadership necessary to unite people because they are the only ones who have the necessary qualities. Your words and actions have proven that you folks have the courage to stand by your convictions.

We certainly hope you folks beat the winter weather in gathering your crops. The children could not agree on one name for the baby calf. Ruby and I would not interfere as we wanted them to think for themselves. They selected a list of four names with the agreement that whichever one your children preferred out of the four would be okay with them. Here are the names: Rapanza (Fredonya heard this one on TV), Anna Bell, Vicki, and Friendship. So, there you are.

We hope you people enjoy the very best in health and spirit through the holiday season and beyond.

We remain yours sincerely,
Mr. & Mrs. David Sims and Family

December 4, 1959

Mr. Dennis Dowdell
South Bend Urban League
724 Western Avenue
South Bend, Indiana

Dear Mr. Dowdell:

On August 20, 1959, we sent you a letter to forward to Mr. David Sims, in regard to his appearance on our "Image: Minorities" program on the Negro in America. The letter was an invitation from Mr. and Mrs. Marilnus Davids of Spring Valley, Minnesota, to visit with them in their home.

Since then, a lively correspondence has sprung up between the two families. Mr. Bob Considine, narrator of the "Image: Minorities" programs is considering the possibility of using this correspondence as the subject for one of his columns in the New York Journal American. In order to do so, he would like to see all the letters which the Sims family received from the Davids family. Mr. Sims has been able to give us all the letters he received with the exception of the first one, (the most important one) which we presume you had forwarded to him. Is it possible that you might have his letter, or a copy, in your files? If so, we would appreciate it if you would send this letter to the Image department, at the above address, and we will see that Mr. Considine gets it.

Thank you for all the cooperation you have shown us in this matter. We look forward to hearing from you in the near future.

Very truly yours,

Peter Lassally
Producer Image Series

PL:nl

cc: Mr. David Sims

31

Obviously, there was some initial hesitancy on both parties to allow Mr. Considine access to their private correspondence. In the end, though, both the Davids and Sims agreed that if used properly, the story of their unique friendship could be the salve that would begin the healing of America's great racial wound. And Considine was just the man to tell that story.

You see, Bob Considine was kind of a big deal at the time. He began his journalism career in 1930 as a tennis correspondent for the now-defunct *Washington Herald.* He later wrote drama reviews and Sunday feature articles for the publication, which was part of a syndicate of major-market daily newspapers owned by media magnate William Randolph Hearst. During World War II, Considine became a war correspondent with the International News Service (also owned by Hearst), the wire service that was a predecessor to United Press International. His column "On the Line" was a popular syndicated feature. Considine even co-authored the best-selling book *Thirty Seconds over Tokyo*, an account of Lt. Col. James Doolittle's 1942 air raid on Japan.[3]

After the war (1955), Considine became a panelist on the television game show *Who Said That?*, hosted on ABC by John Charles Daly. He continued to write his columns, which were now syndicated throughout United Press International. In fact, Considine wrote with a fervor few could match. "Considine's speed, accuracy, and concentration as a writer and his seemingly inexhaustible energy were

---

[3] Bob Considine. (2024, August 26). In Wikipedia. https://en.wikipedia.org/wiki/Bob_Considine

legendary in the newspaper profession. He was known to work at two typewriters at one time, writing a news story on one and a column or book on the other," according to the *Dictionary of American Biography.*[4]

The audacious author had a slew of admirers, from industry heavyweights Rube Goldberg and Nelson A. Rockefeller to three U.S. presidents, receiving accolades from Harry Truman, Dwight Eisenhower, and Lyndon Johnson. Needless to say, someone of Considine's stature could provide quite an audience to whatever subject he chose to write about, so a column in a prominent New York newspaper would potentially bring much attention to the blossoming Sims-Davids friendship. But would the two families appreciate this scrutiny?

---

[4] Finley, John Huston. Dictionary of American Biography. United States: C. Scribner's Sons, 1928.

Chapter 4: Getting to Know You, Getting to Know All About You

Jan. 20, 1960
314 So. Ill. St.
So. Bend, Ind.

Mr. & Mrs. Davids & Family,

Dear friends, we hesitated to write to you folks earlier because we felt that during the holiday season, your family would be occupied and quite busy as we have been. However, in our desire to know how every one of you is getting along, and also to announce the arrival of our ninth offspring, we are taking the liberty once again to correspond with you folks. Sincerely hoping that God has been gracious and merciful to you and yours since we last heard from you. Judging from the photo we received from you during the holiday season, Mr. Davids and the children certainly seem to be enjoying each other. Nothing impresses us more than a happy and content family. We feel they are the backbone of all nations, and yours seems to be one in the happy and content category.

Previously, we had neglected to inquire about a lot of questions that we would appreciate answers to from you folks. First of all, because we have no desire to exhaust or tire you with our long letters, and second, I must confess, I hardly know where to begin. I might add please feel free to ask us any questions that may arise in your mind from time to time. We will gladly answer any and all to the very best of our abilities. We feel that only through trading knowledge can individuals get to know each other.

Before I ask any questions, I'll answer a few. Maybe you folks would like to know how our family got the chance to appear on "Image".

Well, a national organization called the Urban League was selected by NBC to present our people's views on a selection of 40 questions in regards to Negro-White relationships in America. Only four cities were awarded the brotherhood award in 1950. To continue, Mr. Dennis Dowdell, the executive director of the Urban League, selected our family to speak for our city. I was surprised and honored, and so was the family.

We noted with great interest you enjoyed the opportunity of attending Iowa State College. If my memory serves me correctly, that's so wonderful. It's quite an advantage to have an education that you can pass on to your children. Ruby and I have the utmost desire to try and get some technical training in some field. Life is very hard without it. Unfortunately, neither of us graduated from high school, and after accumulating such a large family, money and time that was needed to realize our dream has always been far from us.

What is the population of Spring Valley? Are there any of our people there? If so, what do they do to earn a living? Are your areas noted for industry manufacturing, farming, or mining?

What do you folks do for entertainment and recreation? Does Mr. Davids like to fish? What kind of a youth education program does your church have? Please describe.

In closing, I'd like to say we've been wanting to ask these questions for a long time. Ruby and the baby should return home about the 26th.

May God keep and protect you all until we meet.

Sincerely Yours,
David & Ruby Sims and children

~~~~~~

R. R. #3 - Box 100
Spring Valley, Minn.
January 26, 1960

Dear Mr. & Mrs. Sims and family,

The announcement that another darling baby girl has come to bless your home gave us great joy. Thank you for remembering us with a picture of her.

We also enjoyed your letter, so now I shall try to answer your questions and bring you up to date on what has been going on here at our home. We are enjoying this letter exchange so much and are eagerly anticipating the day when we shall meet.

Now, to answer some of your questions.

As to the population of Spring Valley. I looked at our road atlas, and it shows 2,467 people living there. There aren't any of your people living there, but we are only 20 miles south of Rochester, and there are a number of Negro folks living there. I don't know what occupations they are employed in, but I shall inquire and tell you in my next letter.

This is a very productive agricultural area. We raise corn, soy beans, oats, hay, and clover, and alfalfa pastures for the cows to graze on during warm months.

Our cows are a mixture of breeds, but mostly Guernsey and Short Horn. The Guernsey in them makes them good milkers and the Short Horn are good beef cattle.

We have pigs, a few chickens, just enough for our own eggs, and one horse that we plan to sell soon as its mate was struck and killed by lightning last year.

As to the names for the calves that you sent us, Joyce agrees with Fredonya that Rapanza is a beautiful name for it. We have two more needing names, so we are using Anna Bell and Friendship for them.

We already have a Victoria or Vicky, so we liked that one, too. We thought Friendship was a very nice name.

Along with agriculture, there is quite a lot of industry. I wish I were better informed about it. Perhaps you have heard of the wonderful medical center in Rochester. It is a city full of hotels, motels and restaurants since there are thousands of guests coming and going from there all the time.

Now, as to our family's entertainment and recreation. First of all, we have a very happy time right here at home. Music recreation we enjoy every day. Lots of singing and piano and organ playing. We have a fairly large library of books, and all of us love to read and study. Have you folks ever played scrabble? My husband and I enjoy that a lot. The children have a tricycle, and for Christmas this year, Grandpa & Grandma Attig in Iowa gave the children a swing-slide set, which we will put up in the spring when the weather gets better.

In the summer, we enjoy picnics and trips and all year round we have many house guests and love to go visiting.

Before I was married, I used to go fishing with my dad, but Marienus has never fished and I wasn't good enough to teach him, so we haven't gone since we were married December 24, 1954. Minnesota is good fisherman's country though, so if you enjoy it, we'll plan a day of going to the Mississippi River or Lake City and have a picnic and anyone who cares to fish may do so.

At our last Missionary Society meeting, Rev. Utzman told the group of our growing friendship, and one of my very dear neighbors came to me afterward and said, "Be sure to save a day for us. We want you to have a picnic at our house one day." They have 4 children, so with our 2 and your 9 there should be a playmate for everyone.

We begin our church program for the youth at 2 years of age when they begin Sunday school.

Then at age 12 they also attend a youth fellowship which meets every Sunday evening. Before they join the church, they are thoroughly instructed as to church history, doctrine, and the love of Christ for them and are led to accept Him and His church.

Much of the children's recreation is based on this fellowship at the church. They have wiener roasts, hayrides, Christmas parties, treasure hunts, etc. To earn money for their group they have a car wash Saturday once a year, and pick up corn in the fields that the corn picker has missed.

There is so much to tell that it will probably take a number of letters to share it all with you, but I shall try to do so in future letters.

We were interested in the way you were selected to be on NBC. It was one of the things we had been wondering.

Also, we've been wondering how you plan to come. Will you drive a car, or bus, train, etc.?

We are also wondering when your birthdays are. Mine is May 26, 1930. Marienus' is December 24, 1917 (we were married on his birthday), Joyce is August 25, 1956 and Gregory came to us August 28, 1958. I must close now or the mailman will come and go without me getting this out to the mailbox.

I am hoping, trusting, and praying that we will find some way to help with some of the travel expenses, as we want you to visit us so badly. We're especially happy about the new baby and have a crib all ready for it in the room with its mama and daddy.

So, for now, we wish you God's richest blessings.

Sincerely, your friends,
Marienus, Roselyn, Joyce, and Gregory

Feb. 19, 1960
314 So. Ill. St.
So. Bend, Ind.

Mr. and Mrs. Davids & Family,

Dear Friends, our warmest and most heartfelt greeting of love and friendship we extend to you. As always, we offer advance apologies for the delay in answering your wonderful letter. We are sure you know no neglect is intended, as you folks are constantly in our thoughts. It's difficult for us to find words to describe our feeling of friendship for you folks: your thoughtfulness, your kind acts of friendship, your consideration of others, the warmness of sincerity displayed in your letters are just a few of the qualities that serve to encourage and inspire us to be even more determined that our friendship shall never end. The wonderful gift we received for little Belinda Ann was most welcome. It lifted all of our hearts, just realizing the spirit in which it was given. It was her first. We shall preserve and treasure it as a token of our friendship.

It is needless for us to say you folks have won our hearts. The children want to come now before you have the opportunity to sell the horse. They have been debating as to who was going to get the first ride. When we mentioned the expense of your maintaining the animal, they blasted Ruby and I with the questions, "Can't we go now? Why do we have to wait? Can't they keep the horse until we get there?" We found it quite amusing. It seems so funny to listen to them and observe their reactions. We forgot to compliment little Joyce in our last letter. Everyone here thought how wonderful and nice for her to be able to participate in the Christmas program. All hope she will continue and be successful in her role with wonderful parents such as you to guide her. We are sure she, along with Gregory, will be. Your letter was very informative. We had no knowledge of Rochester or the wonderful content you described. Now we have a better picture of your area.

41

As much as we dislike displaying our ignorance, we must confess as of now we have no knowledge of scrabble. We peeked in the dictionary and discovered it. It sounds intelligent, fun and interesting according to its definition. We will learn it before we come so we will be able to participate in it when we arrive. It is our intention to travel by motorcar when we come if things go as planned. It completely slipped my memory to ask how is the month of August for hay fever sufferers in your state? Ruby suffers considerably with it here during that period. We have no desire to inconvenience you folks, but we are afraid to journey there if the pollen count is up during this period, as Ruby would be at her lowest ebb during this time. Please forgive our thoughtlessness in this vital matter and advise us as to what would be most convenient for you from the month of July on.

Our birth dates are: David Sims Sept. 9, 1927, Ruby June 8, 1927, David III August 29, 1945, Harold Feb. 12, 1947, Charlotte Feb. 6 1948, Carla March 29, 1949, Paul April 18, 1951, Cheryl Jan. 18, 1953, Fredonya Jan. 16, 1954, Avard June 26, 1956, and Belinda Ann Jan. 18, 1960. Our anniversary is April 10.

Our minister, Mr. Dowdell, and others are also making inquiries as to how our friendship is coming along. Everyone is desirous for the best. Only recently, Mr. Dowdell requested that we keep him informed as they are very much interested in the progress of our friendship, also. Ruby, like Mr. Davids, doesn't particularly care for fishing either, but the children and I love it. We were glad to hear your friends also wanted to make our acquaintance when we arrived. Your pastor has to be a wonderful man to teach such love and understanding to his flock. In many areas today, churchmen are being forced to resign for fulfilling their beliefs with true acts of brotherhood.

May God bless and keep you all until we meet.

From the Sims Family

~~~~~~

R. R.#3 — Box 100
Spring Valley, Minn.
March 16, 1960

Dear Christian Friends,

How we have been rejoicing over the information you gave us in your last letter. With your every letter, we look forward to your visit with greater enthusiasm and anticipation of a happy week together this summer.

I'm so glad you mentioned Ruby's hay fever because after talking to several of the folks here who also suffer with it, it seems that July is a much better month than either June or August. It seems there are a number of June grasses which mature and give off pollen, which makes June a difficult time for those allergic to them. Then, in the later part of July and August, there are all sorts of plants maturing, enough to give trouble such as corn pollen, goldenrod, etc. So now, after investigating the situation, we wondered if the week of July 10-17 would be suitable for you.

There is some talk that if we can arrange the date for certain, quite soon, that our Sunday School would wait until your visit to hold its annual Bible School for the children if your children would like to go. I think you will be hearing from Rev. Utzman soon on this. It might provide a means for your children to make friendships with children of their own ages.

Our winter weather is finally arriving now. While I'm writing, there is quite a blizzard going on outside. Marienus and Joyce are in Spring Valley getting the car fixed so I'm preparing a large kettle of mulligan stew (boiling meat, potatoes, carrots, cabbage and onions) which should be warm and filling for them when they get back through the snow.

I guess I should say our Great Grandma Hunter is fixing it. She has been here with us for a week now and we're hoping she will see fit to stay 2 or 3 more.

She is our champion Scrabble player; we have played it a lot since she's been here, and I've only managed to win twice. We really enjoy playing with her. For us here on the farm, Scrabble is sort of a winter game for those snowed-in times. In the summertime, there are usually so many other activities, we don't find too much time for it. However, I think Great Grandma is a year-round fan. She was 80 on March 4, and my mom & dad had a birthday dinner for her where they live in Renwick, Iowa. We were able to attend and she accompanied us home at that time.

We have, in our Woman's Missionary Society, a program of reading. One of the books I have been reading with a lot of interest is a book called "Seeking to be Christian in Race Relations" by Benjamin E. Mays. He points out very clearly that God looks upon all His children as brothers and that man's love for God is inseparable from man's love for man. Therefore, if we say we love God and yet hate our brother, the truth is not in us.

We are so thankful for good Christian folks like you who can continue to love us and pray for us when so many of our race have performed such gross injustices to so many of your race.

Perhaps Christian brotherhood will have to come from individual personal contact such as ours will be this summer.

And now, children, about the horse. Another man also had just one horse and needed ours badly so he could have a team. She (our Doby) was a very gentle horse, but so very wide I'm afraid you would have felt you were split in two after riding her. However, there are several neighbors here who have regular riding horses and if you enjoy it, I'm sure you can get in some horseback riding.

I hope you will be able to be here on at least one Sunday so you can attend services with us and meet our friends in this community.

How is the new baby? Is she gaining weight?

The chorus of Stewartville high school gave an operetta several weeks ago. It was Gilbert & Sullivan's *The Mikado*. I was happily surprised at what a mature performance they gave. Some of our neighbor girls and boys were in it so it was doubly interesting.

Thank you again for your letters and if the dates of July 10-17 are alright for you, then we have only four short months to wait until we shall meet.

Love to you all,
Marienus, Roselyn, Joyce & Gregory

~~~~~~

March 29, 1960
314 So. Ill. St.
So. Bend, Ind.

Mr. and Mrs. Davids and Family,

Dear friends, we received your wonderful letter along with one from your minister, the Rev. Utzman. As a result, we had a double reason for joy. We enjoy very much the letters we receive from you folks. They are enlightening. You folks certainly have a leader you can be proud of. According to his letter, he seems to be equipped with all the qualities of inspiring greatness. His leadership is definitely an asset to your community. You folks are evidence of that.

We informed the Rev. Utzman of our willingness to try and be there the week suggested in your letter. We agreed to accept an offering to share the expenses of our coming after Rev. Utzman stated he felt it would be nice if the church as a whole could have a part in our coming, adding our visit would be such a realistic way in which we can further brotherhood and understanding in racial relations. We felt that if, in his opinion, this was or would be the desire of the congregation, we simply had to accept. Words cannot describe our feeling of joy to know that this kind of spirit prevails among you all. Also, we informed him that the date and arrangement for the annual Bible School would be alright by us.

Your minister spoke very highly of you and Mr. Davids, referring to you folks as wonderful Christians with a love for life and depth. We want to thank you for your effort and the information about the pollen in your area. Mr. Davids is blessed to be able to spend some time with the children. That aids family life and helps develop a closer relationship. My work keeps me from family contact except for weekends, as my job shift is from 3:30 pm to 12 am. I'll have the right to exchange shifts in September.

It certainly is a wonderful thing to include in your missionary society program reading books on various topics. As yet, we have not read "Seeking to be a Christian in Race Relations" by Benjamin Mays, but we shall immediately. We are so glad you mentioned it; otherwise, it would have escaped our attention. The passage you mentioned about man's love for God being inseparable from man's love for his fellow man, as pointed out by Dr. Mays, is so true. The fact is, any man who professes to love God and his righteousness, and at the same time, lives with hate and contempt in his heart for his fellow man, must realize the contradiction.

When you speak of being thankful for our Christian love in spite of the gross injustices imposed upon our people by so many of yours, with the deepest of humility and compassion, we must say that it is we who are thankful for Christians such as you folks. If it were not for the compassion of Christ in you, you would not see the injustices. You would not hear our cry. You would not extend to us a hand of love and friendship. It is only those in Christ who have the ability to see the need that this be done. So, we are sure you understand why we must continue to love and pray that God persevere and prolong the life of all people who seem to stand for his righteousness in this life. Our salvation depends upon each other. Man can live in love and peace or perish with violence and hate. Being the victims of the latter, we know from experience how devastating to humanity it can be. Our constant hope and desire is to live in peace and love with our brothers and show the earth God's creation in happiness.

The children say they will be happy and can hardly wait for the planned visit. Ruby and I are just as anxious.

We'll be glad to attend church service with you. We are sure it will be a heartwarming and wonderful experience for us all.

Belinda is growing by leaps and bounds. Presently, she weighs nine pounds seven ounces.

We are happy to hear of your great-grandparent enjoyment during her visitation with you folks; also, her activity and energy and soundness of mind at her age. It means so much to be able to enjoy a full and rich life.

We would appreciate an opportunity to enjoy a little of the mulligan stew you mentioned when we arrive. It sounds wonderful.

In closing, we'd like to say may God keep and bless you until we meet.

Sincerely with love,
David and Ruby Sims and Family

Sadly, the letter from Rev. Utzman that Mr. Sims referenced could not be accessed to place here, but from his letter to the Davids, it is obvious that the faithful father of nine holds this devout man of God in high regard and is thankful for the generous offer from the Sumner Center church to help defray travel expenses. His response to Rev. Utzman follows.

~~~~~~

March 24, 1960
314 So. Ill. St.
So. Bend, Ind.

Rev. Utzman,

Dear Sir: Your wonderful letter of March 16, in which you extended a welcome hand of Christian fellowship on behalf of your congregation to our family, is most heartwarming and welcomed by all of us. Our spirits have been lifted and our faith increased as a result of your letter exchange with the Davids. Your letter makes us realize even more so why the Davids are true Christians. Your constructive teaching and guidance in religious principle, your expressed desire to further brotherhood and understanding in the area of racial relations, your desire for the church to share our transportation expense, and, more than anything else, your happiness about our forthcoming visit with members of your church serves to further our belief that they had to have an outstanding leader such as yourself to open their hearts and home to our family in the first place. We can only hope and pray that God will enrich your desire and knowledge and preserve and prolong your life, for it is leaders like you that are needed, not only in our nation but all over the world, if mankind is to live in love and peace rather than hate and destruction.

If it is your opinion that it would be the desire of the church to have a part in sponsoring our coming there, then there is no room for our refusal.

We rejoice to know that this kind of spirit prevails; we will gladly accept. You can plan your bible class to correspond with our coming; if all goes well, it is our intention to come during the suggested week. I'm sure the children will get a wonderful experience and enjoyment out of the classes. We agree with you wholeheartedly when you say the Davids are wonderful Christians, full of the love and depth for life their letters display. In our letter exchange, our praise of their quality is directed and intended for both Mr. and Mrs. Davids; we feel that Roselyn expresses their mutual feelings and understanding. May God keep and bless you all.

Sincerely,
David & Ruby Sims & children

R. R.#3 Box 100
Spring Valley, Minnesota
April 29, 1960

Dear Friends,

Spring has at least arrived in Minnesota. It is so welcome this year. Everything is showing signs of new life. Although this is a very late spring, as it is rather cold and we're getting lots of rain, still the grass is green, the trees are budding out, and the robins have arrived back from the south.

Spring also means many new little arrivals on the farm. I wish your children could see them. We have two mother cats, and they have nine little kittens to look after. Five of them are large enough to be roly-poly and playful and Joyce and Gregory love to go to the barn to play with them. The baby chicks are arriving from the hatcheries. They are little puffs of yellow feathers with two little jet-black eyes and make little peep noises.

My letter is late this time as I've been helping Marienus with the new little pigs that have been arriving. We have eight sows this year, and six of them have had their litters. They are having good-sized families. Last night, we spent about an hour in the rain putting a sow in the hog house who had just had nine little pigs out in the yard. We loaded the babies in a bushel basket and put them in a nest of straw and then by means of a panel, got the old mother hog to go be with her family. Sometimes, if little pigs get chilled and don't get some milk right away, we bring them into the house and put them by the stove and feed them with a medicine dropper, and then when they get lively, take them back to the litter.

We are so amused at the little calves when they are let out of the barn to sample some of this spring weather, they race around the barn lot, kick up their heels, and look like they're having a real frolic. Rapunza, Friendship, and Anna Bell are just as frisky as the rest.

Ordinarily, Sharkey would have the oats seeded, but this year because of the late spring, it isn't done yet. However, the grassy seed is purchased and everything is ready to go when the land is ready. Oh yes, "Sharkey" is Marienus's nickname.

The children's grandpa and grandma in Iowa gave them a swing and slide set for Christmas, and we promised Joyce and Gregory that on the first nice day, we would put it together for them. Several days ago, the weather was fine for it, so the children are spending lots of time outdoors now.

Joyce told me the other day she would be glad when "her friends" would come to play on it with her. By "her friends" she means your children, as I carry their pictures in my purse, and she loves to have me get them out so she can see "her friends."

I think there are many happy hearts looking forward to your visit this summer.

We live in what is called Sumner Township. It is a six square mile area, and our church is at or near the center; therefore, it bears the name Sumner Center church. Many of the neighbors are members of this church, and many of the ladies have offered so many things. For example, one wants to make cookies that we hope will make your stay with us most pleasant, as she thinks with our eleven children, we'll be able to use them. The thing that has really thrilled me is that at the last council of administration meeting of the church, they decided they would pay $25.00 of your travel expenses and the money will be here for you when you arrive. We are so eager for your visit that we are already counting the weeks. In just ten weeks, we'll be having Christian fellowship together, the Lord willing.

Did you have a pleasant Easter? Ours was especially nice this year. Joyce colored some eggs; the Easter bunny hid them and also left some candy. Sunday morning, the children had an Easter egg hunt. Then, as we were getting ready for church, a young couple from Iowa, who had just been married the evening before, came and spent the day with us and went to services with us. We had a wonderful time entertaining the newlyweds. Then, also, our choir sang a cantata Easter evening. It was "The Risen King." We also performed it at Rochester and Cherry

Grove. It added much to our Easter worship.

Last Sunday afternoon, we drove to Rochester to visit friends, but they weren't home, so we drove to the airport and watched the airplanes land and take flight. It was such fun and the children were especially delighted.

Yesterday, I went to a meeting of our neighborhood birthday club, and we had a plant, bulb, and seed exchange. I bought some gladiola bulbs, dahlia bulbs, white daisies, and a number of house plant slips for our window boxes. We also discussed plans for a group tour of some of the interesting things in Rochester on May 3. We're all looking forward to that.

I want to get my house cleaning done next week so that when it is time to put in the garden, I'll be ready to do it. I guess you can tell by the way I have talked on and on about spring and its activities that it's my favorite time of the year.

I am enclosing some more pictures which I hope will be of interest to you.

No 1 - was taken on our wedding day Dec. 24, 1954, so I've changed some since then but thought you might like to see it.

No 2 - is Rev. Utzman in the center with Mrs. Utzman and their oldest son Brian. They have another little girl now, Diane, and are expecting a third child this summer sometime. It was taken one evening when they were here on a pastoral call. Sharkey had just come in from chores and Joyce was much smaller than she is now.

No 3 — is a more recent picture taken last September when we were on a trip with Grandmother. The boy with the camera is our nephew, who was stationed in Biloxi, Miss. at that time. He is now in Turkey. I've had my hair cut since then so I look a little different, but not much.

We hope this finds you all happy and well. God has richly blessed our two families and as we continue together in Christian brotherhood and love, we pray we shall continue to do so.

Our love to you all,
Sharkey, Roselyn, Joyce & Gregory Davids

A Blessed Christmas
1959
The Davids
Marienus, Roselyn
Joyce & Gregory

The aforementioned photo No. 1 appears here, as does No. 3. Photo No. 2 is unavailable. In its stead is the 1959 Davids Christmas card mentioned by Mr. Sims in his letter dated January 20, 1960. He observes that "Mr. Davids and the children certainly seem to be enjoying each other." Not so sure about Greg, given his expression, but Joyce's love for her daddy is on full display, and as her husband for 44 years, this author can verify that no daughter revered her father more than Joyce did, once calling him "the most Christ-like man I have ever known."

Chapter 5: An Unexpected Development

Well, spring has sprung and love is in the air, at least for the animals on the Davids farm, given the preponderance of new arrivals. Roselyn, Marienus, and kids are busy with chores but also brimming with excitement as they ready their residence for their much-anticipated visitors from South Bend. But that elation is tempered with concern, as David Sims has not responded to Roselyn's letter from a month and a half ago, very out of character for the effusive ink slinger.

~~~~~~

R. R.#3 Box 100
Spring Valley, Minn.
June 12, 1960

Dear Friends,

Only about 24 days, and the Lord willing, we shall meet. You have been in our thoughts and prayers every day as we happily anticipate your arrival.

Since it's been quite a while since we've heard from you, we wondered if you received our letter written April 29, with the pictures enclosed. Whether you got it or not, we just wanted to drop you a line to say "hello" tonight as we've been thinking of you and discussing sleeping arrangements, etc.

Rev. Utzman called the other day and inquired about the children's ages as he was ordering bible school materials and wanted to secure the correct supplies for the children.

We telephoned the South Bend operator tonight. We thought maybe we could visit for a few minutes; however, she couldn't find a phone listed under your name. Is there some phone where you can be reached? Our phone number is Racine 2488.

We thought you should know in case you wanted to call for directions to our place. So many people try to get us through Spring Valley exchange and are unable to reach us as Racine is our phone and Spring Valley is our address.

We are enclosing a portion of a Minnesota map to help you locate us. Highway 16 comes to Spring Valley, and the best way to reach us is to continue about 5 miles west of Spring Valley to the junction of 16 and 63 – then north on 63 to Racine then, I shall draw a map for you from Racine to our home.*

We always direct everyone here from Racine as the road here from Spring Valley is very, very winding and hard to follow.

Will you be coming the 8th, 9th, or 10th of July? If we know the day, we can leave the yard light burning until you arrive, if it should be in the evening. Do you plan to make the trip all in one day? Our prayers go with you as you travel for a safe journey here.

And so, we look forward to our forthcoming visit.

Our love,
Marienus, Roselyn, Joyce & Gregory

* The map was drawn on the letter sent to the Sims but not the copy Roselyn kept.

~~~~~~

June 15, 1960
314 So. Ill St.
South Bend, Ind.

Mr. and Mrs. Davids.

Dear friends, since we last wrote you, many unexpected and despairing events have taken place. A few months ago, we were out on strike at my place of employment. Employees lost about five hundred dollars in wages. And after we returned to work, we only worked four days a week. I am sure you know after a few months, our savings were used to maintain our living expenses. We hesitated to write you in the hope that somehow, someway, even at this late date, our family could visit with you. Needless to say, you must know how heartbroken everyone is at this time. Industrial employment is so uncertain, and the cost of living so high that one cannot tell what to expect next. Even as I write this letter, I don't know if the corporation will lay off next week or not. We are having a meeting on it at 1:00 PM today. If the company decides to close for model change, it will be a month earlier than last year. This could mean another twelve hundred dollars in wages lost to most of us as the new model will not be on the market until early September.

Please explain to Rev. Utzman and others we had every intention of coming. Express our sincere regrets about all the plans being spoiled. We certainly hope and pray the preparation expenses haven't been too great for you all. Again, I must say, words cannot express our heartfelt sorrow at this time. The realization of all the anticipation, planning, and expectation on the part of you folks grieves us the most.

Last year, my earning was close to $5000. This year, if I'm able to earn $3500, it will surprise me. The past four months have distressed our family considerably. Our minister will write soon. We hesitated to bring him up to date because of recent illness and death in his family. We felt it unwise to approach him during his grief.

We received your wonderful letter of April 29. As I said previously, we delayed answering in the hope that our predicament would improve to the extent that we would be able to forward to you our plans of departure, arrival, etc.

The photo of you, Mr. Davids, your minister and others was well received by all. They brought much joy into our home. We enjoy looking at them.

Spring is also our favorite season of the year. We did not overlook your birthday at this time. Everyone sends greetings and hopes God blesses you with many more to come. We had some photos made, but as yet, the film has not been developed. In our next letter, we definitely will enclose a couple of snapshots of Ruby and myself.

Please accept our apologies for the overdue letters. Our desire to be able to come so badly inspired us to hope for a miracle rather than face the facts.

We remain yours in Christ.

Sincerely with all our love,
David and Ruby Sims and children

~~~~~~

So, the first major setback to the Davids' efforts to host the Sims family comes via a financial hardship. Of course, both parties are extremely dejected yet remain resolute that the coming together of these two God-fearing families is destined to be. What Roselyn and David already know - but are again reminded of - is that the Lord's plans are not necessarily their plans and that if he ordains them, they will happen on his time and terms, not theirs.

July 2, 1960
314 South Ill. St.
South Bend, Ind.

Mr. and Mrs. Davids,

Dear friends, each time we hear from you folks, our
hearts rejoice with gladness. Every letter lifts
our spirits and increases our desire to meet all of
you so very much. Without saying it, we are sure
you know we want very much to be able to fellowship
with you. You folks have given us so much: the
hospitality of your home, your church, money, etc.
Indeed, you have opened your hearts and showered
our family with love and friendship. For these acts,
we shall forever feel indebted. The wonderful offer
made by the unknown interested party mentioned in
your letter makes us feel like casting everything
aside and coming anyway. It is a golden opportunity,
a once-in-a-lifetime chance that our family would
like to be able to accept. However, we hope it is
not too difficult for you folks to understand. As
was stated previously, the strike and part work
week disrupted everything for us. Not only were our
savings used, we also fell behind in our debts.
Being an hourly wage earner in a factory and living
in the city where you must purchase everything you
use in life can be very difficult. An auto worker's
livelihood depends on cars being sold. The company
where I'm employed did not do so well this year. As
a result, we are in a worse predicament this year
than last year at this time.

Even though you folks have done everything humanly possible to see that we would have a safe and secure journey to your community, at this time, it breaks our hearts to realize even with your aid, we cannot come at present. Our family obligation demands our presence here. You can rest assured as soon as we can come, you will be informed. I requested time off from my work in January for the visit with you folks. At that time, we had no way of knowing about the short work week.

To my knowledge, the company has no information about our planned visit with you. At the time I asked for time off, I did not say for what purpose.

We are so glad you left the invitation open. We cannot describe our heartfelt sorrow for not being able to come, knowing everyone expected us. In our grief, we pray God's blessing upon you and wait for and look forward to the day that we shall meet.

As yet, the friend who snapped the photo of us has not had the film developed. Because we want to relieve your mind, we are rushing this letter back. Due to time again, we cannot enclose the snapshot of the rest of the family. I won't say when we will forward them for fear of not being able to keep my word. As soon as possible, we will send them so you all can see the remainder of the family.

We would like to hear from you at your earliest convenience.

We remain yours in Christ, with All Our Love,
David and Ruby Sims and Children

In this last letter, Mr. Sims references the "open invitation" and "money" that may have been already donated, or at least offered, by the church or the Davids family. Since there is no reply from Roselyn to the first of these two Sims missives, it is likely that some correspondence is missing. Every effort has been made to secure all communiqués between the two families, but, going forward, it would seem that one or more letters from Mrs. Davids are absent. Keep in mind that this was 1960 and, living in rural Minnesota, she did not have access to copy machines or mimeographs. As such, she wrote two identical letters – one she sent to the Sims and one she kept for herself.

All letters published here from Mrs. Davids are her copies. Hence, it is quite possible that some of them have gone missing. In such situations, attempts will be made to "fill in the gaps" with knowledge acquired through additional research. In this case, the proposition was indeed left open for the Sims to visit the Davids farmstead, no matter how far off in the future. At this point, no money had yet exchanged hands, though an offer from the church was on the table to assist the Sims, should they find the means to come.

~~~~~~

17W 484 Nimitz Drive
Villa Park, Illinois
August 23, 1960

Dear Friends,

Just a note this morning from Villa Park, where we arrived last night to spend a week with my sister and family.

After looking at a map this morning, we noticed we are probably only about 100 miles from you folks, and if you would be home Friday, the 26th of August, we thought we might drive to South Bend so that we might meet you folks and visit for a few hours.

I can't tell you how disappointed we were when you weren't able to come to our place this summer. Our children could hardly wait to play with their friends from Indiana.

If you would write us at this address, we would know then whether this visit is convenient for you at this time. If you have other plans, please let us know, but if you plan to be home, we shall meet soon.

Hope to hear from you soon. Bye for now.

Love,
Marienus, Roselyn, Joyce, & Gregory

~~~~~~

The Davids and Sims are both heartbroken about not being able to spend time together this summer. But Mrs. Davids has an alternate plan for the two families to finally meet. The ball is now in Mr. Sims' court...

8-24-60
314 So. Illinois St.
So. Bend, Ind.

Mr. & Mrs. Davids and Family,

We cannot express how happy we were to hear that you were so close to our home. We are so glad to know that you can spare a few hours with us. However, we would like to let you know that for the past week or so, we have had a little virus in the family. It's nothing serious, just a sore throat and high temperatures. It only lasted about two to three days at the most. We're explaining this to you because of the children. We felt we should let you know, but we're hoping this won't spoil our chance of seeing each other. We don't want to spoil our chance of meeting each other because we feel we have already met. We have only to see and to be together and enjoy each other.

Here are a few sketches that will help you find our house. If you are taking the toll road, you will come off US 31, which is Michigan St. to Western Ave. west to Illinois St. North. 4th house on the right-hand side. Now, if you're coming 12-20, which runs into 2, which is also Western Ave., you follow the same directions.

I guess we will close until we see you. May God bless & watch over you through your safe journey here.

David, Ruby, & Children

This is my neighbor's phone if you should have need
to call. A+ - 8 - 6747. Mrs. Gerry Harris.

~~~~~~

So, barring any setback with the health of the Sims children, the long-awaited rendezvous between the Sims and Davids may finally take place... just not in the way either family envisioned.

Chapter 6: At Last, They Meet

The day has finally arrived when the two families will meet face-to-face. Friday, August 26th, begins with the entire Davids family plus one (Roselyn's Grandma Hunter) leaving Roselyn's sister's home in Villa Park, Illinois and tootling off to South Bend in their Studebaker. Though the trek was only 100 miles, keep in mind that in 1960, the interstate highway system was still in its infancy, so the route they traversed would have consisted of 2-lane roads, likely paved but poorly maintained. Couple that with the tendency for vehicles of that era to break down often, and you have a recipe for a potentially arduous journey. But the intrepid couple arrived safe and sound at the Sims residence and, no doubt were greeted with hugs, handshakes, and hearty hellos. The two families visited for much of the day in David and Ruby's humble abode, with various neighbors and nearby relatives dropping by to meet this enigmatic white family that the Sims knew only through written correspondence. It is obvious from Mr. Sims' next letter that, despite their reservations, all who visited 314 South Illinois Street were won over by the genuine affection and sincerity displayed by the Spring Valley visitors. Though the Davids stayed but a few hours, their impact on all who met them would be long-lasting and be spoken of for years to come.

314 So. Ill. St.
So. Bend, Ind.
Sept. 13, 1960

Mr. and Mrs. Davids:

Dear friends, we waited until this time to write you so we could include the copies of the Michiana News with our wonderful thoughts of you wonderful people. We certainly hope you folks had a pleasant and safe journey home. You have been in our thoughts ever since you departed. You folks won the hearts of all our friends. Everyone inquired why we didn't get to their home with our friends, referring to you folks, of course. We were delighted to receive so many welcoming and good comments in regard to your short stay. Ruby's uncle was angry because we forgot, in our haste to show you as much of the city as possible, to bring you to his home. He wanted so much to meet you folks, also.

Mr. Walker, the publisher, made several mistakes in the write-up, as you probably have observed. You folks can fill in the correct details and explain to the folks in your area. I'll ask Mr. Walker to correct the print in next month's issue. It's too late now.

Ruby and the children say "hello," and we all hope you are doing well.

My job at Studebaker Corp. was terminated Aug. 31, 1960, so I'm without an income at present, with the exception of $36.00 per week unemployment compensation provided by the state. At present, the future looks very uncertain. However, we are sacrificing. I enrolled in school and started classes Monday night of this week. I'm studying basic electricity as a trade and continuing my high school subjects. I have three courses: American Gov't, English III, and High School Math, as recommended as a start by the councilor. As you know, you can only accumulate eight credits a semester, as I stopped in my sophomore year. I must go over the courses again, which means it will take 3 years to get a diploma if I can keep up with my studies and four additional years of college.

At present, we don't have the slightest idea of how I'm going to get this education, but we are determined to see it through. As we see it, we're lost completely without it anyway. In present-day society, one cannot earn a living in the city without a degree, so even though I'll be forty, and it will be 1967 before I graduate, we feel we owe it to the children to try and accomplish this task.

How are your grandmother and the children doing, and your husband, of course? We certainly hope they are fine. We would appreciate hearing from you folks at your earliest convenience. And we hope the next time you visit, we will be able to afford a larger home and be able to accommodate you with sleeping quarters so that your stay will be more pleasant and longer. As Ruby stated in her letter previously, we felt even before we met that we knew you folks through the sincerity, love and true friendship shown in your letters. We sincerely feel that ours is a friendship of common bonds and ties that nothing can destroy. Our common love for God's righteousness and our fellow man, sincerity, pureness of heart, and the love for all mankind are things that cannot be faked. A feeling of closeness and togetherness is our desire; to reach the ultimate goals of mankind is indeed the tie that binds us forever. You folks can't begin to realize how overjoyed we are to be able to consider you as true friends. It is a depth beyond description; our hearts go out to you. We hope and live with an immediate desire to be able to be in your presence again soon. It is our utmost desire to see you all again. We enjoyed your company so very much. We'd like to hear from you soon.

All send love.
David and Ruby Sims & Children

A few things of note here: the *Michiana News* Mr. Sims alluded to was a publication out of South Bend serving northern Indiana and southern Michigan. Not a newspaper per se, its look and feel were more like that of a program you would buy at a major theater production or sporting event, replete with ads promoting businesses, churches, and events in the bi-state area. Article content included local news, accomplishments of high-profile denizens, editorials, and even political promotions. Its subject matter often highlighted issues important to the Black community.

Sadly, the particular issue Mr. Sims references is not the issue seen here, as it does not contain the article he speaks to. The *Michiana News*, at least in this format, has long been discontinued and efforts to find archived copies were unsuccessful. What this issue does have, however, is an article written by David Sims in which he rails against local authorities for refusing to budget sufficient funds to remedy the horrible conditions in Lasalle Park, the mostly Black neighborhood in which the Sims and so many of their friends reside. Despite the deplorable condition of the roads and utilities servicing this area, the almost all-white city council refused to include ANY monies in the budget for said improvements, prompting Mr. Sims to write a scathing rebuke. It cannot be reprinted here, as permission to do so was never granted; however, it will be addressed further in Chapter 8.

While there appears to be no detailed account of all that transpired on that fateful Friday at the Sims' home, an article published in the Rochester Post-Bulletin does make reference to the epochal occasion.

David Pennington writes, "... while the Davids were visiting her sister in Villa Park, Ill., Mrs. Davids realized they were only about 100 miles away from the Sims' home. So, they drove down on August 26th, received a royal welcome, and met many of the Sims' friends while spending the day there.

After their meeting, Mrs. Davids said she realized that the Sims were 'our kind of people. They displayed no bitterness or hatred for some injustices they had received at the hands of white people. Mrs. Sims told me that hatred is poison and it only poisons those who hate.'"[5]

And speaking of the perspicacious parent of nine, the above letter references one that Ruby must have written to Roselyn, separate from David's communiqués. Since it could not be located, speculation is required as to its content, though it likely involved Ruby waxing poetic about the sincere and genuine friendship the two families had forged, only to be reinforced once they finally met.

Regarding Mr. Sims' pursuit of a high school degree and perhaps even college, his higher education exploits will be addressed in future correspondence.

---

[5] Pennington, David. "Sumner Center White Family, South Bend Negroes Try Human Relations Experiment." Rochester Post-Bulletin, July 7, 1961.

R. R. #3 Box 100
Spring Valley, Minn.
November 3, 1960

Our dear friends,

I'm so ashamed of myself for not writing sooner to
send you the money for the 4 copies of March 24,
1960, which we received in September. The picture
was especially good, we thought. We kept one copy
and gave the other three to Grandma Hunter, Rev.
Utzman, and my sister. They were all so happy to
get them.

Next, we want to congratulate you all for the plans
you have made in the field of education. I know
that, at times, it will seem almost too difficult
to pursue, but after meeting you, we know you will
put forth a determined effort to accomplish your
goal.

One reason for our delay in writing is that we have
been trying to think through some plans where we,
as your friends, might lend an assist to your plans.
As I was bringing in the fall harvest from the
garden, I was wishing there was some way we could
share these foodstuffs, and then an idea began to
form in my mind.

If it would help, we would be happy to have two of
your children come and take their schooling here in
Spring Valley. I think we could manage to pay their
school expenses (book rentals, lunch money, etc.),
and this would not be charity in any sense of the

word, so if David and Harold came, they could assume
such family farm chores as our own children will
assume when they reach that age. Or if the two
eldest girls came, they could help me with the
chickens and play with Joyce & Gregory while I teach
music here at home. We would care for them like
our own.

I know this will take much prayerful consideration
on your part, as it already has on ours. I think
the second semester begins sometime in January, so
you have some time to consider this matter. We know
what a major decision this will be for your family,
and whatever your answer may be, yes or no, be sure
that we understand. I think both of you look upon
your children, as we do on ours - as God's richest
gifts to us - and will consider carefully what is
in the best interest of their future.

Yesterday, we received in the mail the pictures from
our visit with you folks. May we say that your
hospitality was most gracious, and we shall always
treasure the memories of the day we spent with you.
The drive around South Bend and meeting your friends
was so nice. When you see them again, give them
our greetings and let those we missed seeing know
we shall look forward to meeting them at some future
date.

The evening meal was so tasty. We all remarked on
how well everything was prepared, and the fellowship
around the table was most enjoyable.

In the boxes, which should have reached you by now,
are the two rugs which Grandma Hunter wanted you to
have to express her appreciation for your grand
hospitality. The clothing is from some that my
sister-in-law handed down to me. I gave some to my
friends here and picked out some things I thought
your girls might use and sent them along to you.

I must close now and get this into the mail before
the mailman comes.

Our love to you all.
Marienus, Roselyn, Joyce & Gregory

It is patent that Roselyn and Sharkey are still basking in the glow of
the memories they cherish from their August encounter and are
thankful for the "gracious hospitality" shown them, so much so that
gifts of rugs and clothing were mailed to the Sims. Roselyn mentions
receiving "the pictures from our visit with you folks." Some
photographs dated August 1960 are most likely what she is
referencing and are included below. The "4 copies of March 24,
1960" likely refer to the copies of the Michiana News sent by Mr.
Sims, although the date on the pictured copy is different. What
became of the March 24th copies is unknown. That said, the biggest
takeaway from this letter is the Davids' proposal to ease the Sims'
pecuniary predicament by housing and educating two of their older
children for a time, yet another demonstration of this couple's
benevolent Christian spirit. Will the Sims accept such a generous
offer, given its ramifications?

Top row left to right: David Jr., David III, Charlotte, Paul.

Center: Ruby, holding baby Belinda.

Front row left to right: Cheryl, Avard, Fredonya

Missing: Harold, Carla Diane

Avard and Greg play in the Sims' backyard.

Grandma Hunter holding baby Belinda.

Other photos from that historic occasion are either lost, fuzzy, or faded over the years so as to be unusable, including those with Davids family members, so one is included here of the foursome on their farm shortly after returning from their South Bend excursion.

Chapter 7: Holiday Blues and Family News

314 So. Ill. St.
Nov. 21, 1960
So. Bend, Ind.

Dearest friends, please forgive the long delay in answering your wonderful letter. It is extremely difficult for one to retain one's sanity during these trying times when the constant threat of starvation and having no income to meet the necessities of life, such as shelter, etc. daily stare you in the face, posing a problem that is almost beyond imagination. Please don't feel depressed when we acquaint you with our problem. We have no desire whatsoever to do that. We share, truthfully, our economic plight only because we hope you can gain further insight into the true status of the majority of our people in this land.

The offer you folks made to assume the responsibility of two of our offspring brought Ruby and myself to tears. We have known and felt you folks' sincerity and pureness of heart by your kind acts and deeds. Your every letter enriches our love and trust to the bursting point. If the world could display the humility and the sharing and sacrificing of material wealth and spiritual love that you have shown us, there would be no need for a United Nations. Man would live in love and peace for the betterment of all mankind. This would be the ultimate goal that our society could reach.

We know you understand when we say we can't find words to describe how wonderful it makes us feel to have friends such as you. We can think of no other persons we would rather have our children associate with than you folks. Your many letters and short visits aided in convincing us even more how much love, kindness, understanding and devotion you have to share with others. The community of Spring Valley should pray that God preserves the magnificent quality displayed by you folks. In as much as we would like to have our children enjoy a more secure home with all the advantages, we know you have to give and feel you would give unselfishly and devotionally. Ruby and I feel that we must somehow, with the aid of God, keep the family unit together. Our children are our life, and their presence serves to give us inspiration and even more courage to struggle for the ultimate goal of all mankind: to leave them with the spirit of love and righteousness for God and his fellow man. This heritage is all we have to give, and we feel that this is stamped in their hearts. Future generations will benefit from it, just as we have from folks such as you.

Tell Grandma to please forgive me for forgetting her name. I know it's not Attig. I recall asking you that when you were here. Anyway, Ruby loved the rugs, as we all did, and she must learn the secrets of making them. We don't have to tell you (as we are sure you know) how much both packages of clothing that we received were needed and appreciated.

Must close. Answer soon as we desire very much to hear from you soon.

Love from all,
David, Ruby, and Children

PS: Enclosed is a photo Mr. Walker gave us. If you like, make a copy and return it to us. It is the only copy we have.

~~~~~~

It is evident from the tone and verbiage of Mr. Sims' most recent epistle that his family's situation is dire. Despite this, they do not accept the Davids' offer, citing the benefits of keeping the family together, which outweigh any monetary relief that might accrue from consenting to the proposal.

Additionally, the aforementioned photo supplied by Mr. Walker is MIA, as could very well be pieces of correspondence from Mrs. Davids (her next included letter is dated May 1, 1961), which are referenced in the following letters from Mr. Sims, in which he brings holiday well-wishes, gratitude, family news, and concern for the Davids family, as Roselyn seemingly hasn't answered David's communiqués in a timely manner.

314 So. Ill. St.
South Bend, Ind.
January 20, 1961

Dear friends,

You folks remain in our thoughts constantly. We received your season's greetings, the gift, and the birthday greetings. The children were extremely happy, as we all rejoiced. We always look forward to and anxiously await your letters. It warms our hearts to know that our acquaintance maintains a bond of thoughtfulness, love, and friendship, qualities that can only come from the soul. It is our desire for you folks to know that nothing will ever destroy that bond. We want so much to warm your hearts as you have warmed ours.

Although unemployment is very high in our area (actually critical), it is our desire to visit you this year. It was heartbreaking and quite disappointing not to be able to make it last year. But then you came. If only we had more room and you folks had more time, I'm sure we would have been able to enjoy each other even more.

We mailed a Christmas card to your grandmother in Iowa, thanking her for the gift. You can't picture how we felt to receive a gift from her. It brought us to tears. We asked her to write; however, we haven't heard from her. We wonder if she received the card. Have you heard from her lately? We certainly would like to know if she received our appreciation.

Belinda is walking quite well now. I don't recall if she was or not when you folks were here. The children all send their love and greetings to Joyce, Gregory, and all of you. Ruby sends her best wishes for health and happiness, and, of course, I'm included in this. The children were happy to know that, again, Joyce participated in the Christmas program. They did, as well, at their school. Also, a Methodist youth fellowship group gave them various presents and invited them to a pageant. It was wonderful. I went along to observe. It is customary for religious groups to assist large, needy families during the holiday season with food, toys, etc. Someone turned in our name, and the fact that I was unemployed is why we received the blessing, and it was a blessing, indeed.

We must close now. Please forgive us for not knowing definitely that the gift came from you. We had no way of knowing as we did not receive your card until several days later. Answer soon.

With all our love,
David and Ruby Sims & children

~~~~~~

Dear Friends,

We are very much concerned as to why we haven't heard from you. Is everyone OK?

We received the wonderful gift sent from Minneapolis. We assumed you folks sent it. There

was no return address on it. Also, your wonderful
Grandma in Iowa sent us a lovely card and gift. We
pray God's blessings on all of you outstandingly
wonderful people. Please forgive our boldness when
we say we are concerned as to why we haven't heard
from you. As you know, our utmost desire is to
remain permanently real friends. By your kind acts,
you have gained our love, our thoughts and concerns,
and our friendship for life. We desire very much
to hear from you within the near future.

Sincerely, with our Deepest Love,
Ruby, David, and the Children

The previous message appeared in this undated Christmas card, undoubtedly sent in December of '60 or January of '61. Note that Ruby's name appears first, perhaps an indication that she authored this Yuletide note of thanks and concern, though the style is very much David's.

February 9, 1961
314 So. Ill. St.
South Bend, Ind.

Dear friends,

I hope all of you are getting along fine. We are doing just fine. Everyone said for me to tell all of you hello. My sisters, Charlotte, Cheryl, Fredonya, and Belinda, wanted to thank you all for the money and the card. And we would like to know your birthdays, too. Will you send them to us, please, so we can give all of you a card?

My sister is going to be on television - her whole class is. I wish all of you could have seen her. I am going to tell my mother and father to send all of you a Valentine's card to thank you all for the nice cards all of us have received.

I guess I'd better be closing now.

From Diane & family

P.S. Don't forget to send us the dates of all of your birthdays.

Not to be outdone by her prolific father, Carla Diane decided to put pen to paper and thank the Davids personally - from her and her sisters - for cards and money sent by Roselyn, most likely for their birthdays.

Speaking of thankfulness, at least one of the Sims' neighbors was also a recipient of the generosity of the Sumner community by way of David and Ruby. This neighbor was so overcome with gratitude, she wrote Roselyn a letter expressing her appreciation for the gifts.

It is highly likely that the Sims shared the largesse from the Racine samaritans with many local friends and it is quite possible that others may have sent the Davids letters of thanks, but this is the only one in the possession of yours truly.

~~~~~~

3-17-1961

To the community of Racine,

I am writing a few lines to thank you all for the clothing Mrs. Sims gave us that came from you all. I sure do thank you all for them. They were nice.

I am the mother of 13 children. My husband had been out of work, too, but we are working now. As you can see, I was glad to have them. We know the Sims well. I have two daughters who are not at home. One is going to college and will finish in 24 more weeks. The other is taking typing. I am proud of them. I have another that will finish high school in June. I am trying all I can to get every one of them through high school. I will have three in high school this year, six in grade school, and two at home.

I asked Mrs. Sims would she ask you to come by my house when you are here again. She said you all were sure nice people so I would like to meet you all. The only way to behave is to be nice to one another.

Well, I guess that's all I can say. May the Lord bless you all until we meet.

Mrs. Blake

Chapter 8: A True Social Justice Warrior

The next piece of correspondence, chronologically, requires a prelude.

David Sims was the de facto spokesperson for the Black community in his area. Despite his limited formal schooling (tenth-grade education), his well-crafted letters-to-the-editor in local publications and outspokenness at city council meetings earned Sims a reputation as one who would speak the truth, regardless of the consequences. His brash, courageous approach to shining a light on the plight of his brethren did not go unnoticed. When the Urban League was tasked by Mr. Lassally to find someone who would artfully and candidly articulate the problems faced by poverty-stricken Black households, Sims was chosen. As his petitions to local officials fell on deaf ears, David embarked on the next logical course of action: he wrote to President Kennedy about the problems faced by unemployed Black men and their families in South Bend! What follows is his letter to this country's chief executive.

~~~~~~

April 10, 1961

Mr. President:

Our family of eleven, being a part of the 5 ½ million unemployed workers in America and a part of the seventeen million who go to bed hungry every night, feel impelled out of absolute necessity for our survival on the face of this earth to write in the hope that you can give immediate aid to our acute economic plight (actually a starvation diet).

89

Mr. President, each member of our family receives exactly $13.21 per month (30 days) for food. This includes approximately $18.00 in federal surplus foods given to relief recipients by the overseer of the poor in the city of South Bend, Indiana. Reliefers are told by local government officials that present budgets will not permit an increase in the allowance for our existence diet. We cannot exist on the present amount allowed and are forced to appeal constantly to private charities for food supplements two weeks out of every month. Our family has been informed by private charities that their budget will not permit a repeat of supplementary monies for diets. Needlessly, I tell you our family must go hungry for days. Unemployment is extremely acute in our area. Our county and local officials cannot and do not supply our immediate food needs. We realize your tremendous task as President of the United States is a gigantic responsibility, leaving you little time for individual family needs and desires. But our faith and belief is that you are concerned about the needs and desires of every American, especially so when this need is food to prevent starvation or death from malnutrition. Sincerely, Sir, when we say people are hungry in the city of South Bend, we speak from actual experience.

Unless immediate aid is forthcoming, many of us may not be around to receive what has been promised. All we ask is the opportunity to earn our keep. If

that is not possible immediately, can you relieve
our being forced to go hungry in this land of
abundance?

We anxiously await your reply. Hundreds of
unemployed families with children need food
desperately in our city today.

Sincerely,
David Sims and Family
314 S. Illinois Street,
South Bend, Indiana

~~~~~~

Whether or not this eloquent plea for assistance attained an audience
with the US commander-in-chief was never established. It was
apparently received and then forwarded to a federal welfare office,
which contacted Mr. Sims and suggested that he reach out to state
and/or local agents. Of course, David had already done this
numerous times, all to no avail. While certain officials did sympathize
with his plight, no actions beneficial to Sims or the families he
represented were ever documented to have occurred.

Sims' writing prowess is further exemplified in an article, clipped
from an unspecified newspaper, entitled "Action Wanted", which
somehow found its way into the collection of correspondence
between the two beneficent families. While it has no date, the
references to President Kennedy and then Governor Matt Welsh, who
served Indiana from 1961-1965, would indicate its publishing to be in
accordance with this timeline. Whether it was written before or after
the letter to President Kennedy is unspecified.

"It is extremely disheartening and significant to note that while our national government is doing its utmost to stabilize our economy and grant educational opportunities to the various states in this union, our elected state representatives and senators either were asleep or deliberately ignored the needs of hundreds of thousands of Indiana citizens.

I am referring to the children's aid bill recently signed into law by President Kennedy to relieve the suffering of children of unemployed mothers and fathers. According to the news release in the Tribune, provisions are made to reimburse a major share of the cost of state-administered relief to needy families.

With relief costs soaring in distressed communities, one would think our state officials would be overjoyed to grasp the opportunity to share relief costs with the federal government. This would relieve the drain on our already overburdened community tax budget and, at the same time, maintain a well-fed and healthy citizenry. Indeed, I question the sincerity, integrity, abilities, and capacities of these entrusted officials to administer the responsibilities of this state's welfare.

Gov. Welsh stated our state will be unable to participate in the program because the legislature did not enact a state-enabling law. There is no excuse for this gross error on the part of so many.

How do they dare flout their moral obligations and legal duties of preserving the health and welfare of the future citizens of this sovereign state? As one of the hundreds of thousands of able-bodied, unemployed fathers, I appeal to Gov. Welsh to call a special session of the state legislature for the specific purpose of enacting a state-enabling law so that this state can become a participant. Hundreds of thousands of defenseless, ill-fed, ill-clothed children cry out for aid today."

~~~~~~

As previously stated, the *Michiana News* article written by Mr. Sims could not be included in its entirety. That said, Sims' invocation for aid, along with some poignant questions he raises, are worthy of mention. Recall that monies were desperately needed in the Lasalle area to improve roads, many of which were dirt. A common practice at the time was to "oil" the roads to keep down the dust. Sims and other Lasalle residents requested that they be paved. This appeal was denied, of course, providing a title for the article: "When Residents Ask for Concrete, Mayor Gives Oil Instead." Hard as it is to imagine, some neighborhoods in Lasalle Park had outdoor restrooms and no sewer or gas lines. Sims and his bevy of petitioners aimed to remedy this, but funding was denied, the excuse being that it would be too costly. Sims pointed out that, after allocating monies for the existing budgetary items slated for improvement, there remained $40,000 of uncommitted funds. Despite this, Mayor Voorde remained steadfast in his denial of the request, prompting Sims to ask when the citizens of Lasalle Park would ever get relief, as no improvements had even been considered by the city government for the last four decades despite the dire need and the mayor's promises while campaigning to address such. Sims asked why the Blacks who urged Lasalle residents to vote for Voorde have gone silent and why the members of the mayor's "Black Cabinet" remain tight-lipped. Do they have "hush your mouth" jobs? But Sims, ever the optimist, did not despair; rather, he beseeched others to join the cause of the "Negro leadership" and promised to "redouble our efforts" to bring justice to the Lasalle residents.[6]

---

[6] David Sims, "When Residents Ask for Concrete, Mayor Gives Oil Instead," Michiana News, August 1960.

Chapter 9: The Storm Before the Calm

R. R. #3 Box 100
Spring Valley, Minn.
May 1, 1961

Dear David, Ruby, & family,

Please forgive us for being so late with this letter. Each day, you are in our thoughts and prayers. We are so in hopes that you will be able to make a visit here this summer. Rev. Utzman was wondering if you would have any idea as to the exact time you could come, as he would like to be here to visit with you, also. He doesn't want to be away on vacation during your stay.

Two weeks ago, I attended a county meeting of the Fillmore County United Church Women. They were looking into the possibilities for constructive acts that any of us might do to promote peace and understanding throughout our communities, our country, and our world. I shared with them the happy relationship we have been sharing with you folks, and they want to help sponsor our visit in a financial way.

Our church has set aside $25 for transportation whenever you feel you can journey here.

April 25 - 28, our church made it possible for me to attend the state convention of the Women's Society of World Service held at Farmington,

Minnesota. One of our speakers was Dr. Lowell Gess, a medical missionary to Sierra Leone, Africa. I talked with him, and he said friendships like the one we have been developing would help Christian missionaries so very much, as it is very difficult to explain Christian love when in the missionary's home country, there is so much injustice, as exemplified by the actions of Little Rock's Orval Faubus.

Everyone I speak with seems to feel our planned week together will be a real contribution to understanding that God has many children, and it must grieve him when those children are unkind to each other.

We shall never be able to forget the fine hospitality you showed us while in South Bend.

We are concerned as to what the job opportunities are just now in South Bend. Were you able to continue with your studies?

How are all of the lovely children? I suppose Belinda is in that exploring walking stage by now, isn't she?

An elderly lady here in our community had a number of skirts that her granddaughters had grown out of. She wondered if I knew of anyone who might use them. I hope your sweet girls perhaps can use them. Do they have an opportunity to take home economics in their school?

We shall be eagerly awaiting your decision as to when we will spend a week together. Thank you for your friendship. Our love & prayers are always with you.

Sincerely,
Marienus, Roselyn, Joyce, & Gregory

~~~~~~

As is evidenced by the substance of this letter, the munificent matriarch of the Davids family was not content to merely speak out against racial discrimination; she actively worked toward remediation, citing "the actions of Little Rock's Orval Faubus" as evidence of injustice that had to be vanquished. As many readers may not be familiar with these events, providing background would be prudent.

Orval Faubus was the governor of Arkansas from 1955-1967, serving six consecutive two-year terms. As a progressive Democrat, Faubus supported the "separate but equal" doctrine as handed down by the "Plessy vs Ferguson" Supreme Court case of 1896. But "Brown vs the Board of Education" changed all that in 1954, outlawing segregation by race in public schools. This ruling was highly controversial at the time and led to many clashes - some violent - between opposing forces. One such incident occurred on September 2, 1957, as several Black students attempted to attend the Little Rock Central High School. Making good on his promise while running for Arkansas' highest political office that "no school district will be forced to mix the races as long as I am governor of Arkansas", he deployed the National Guard, who blocked the school's entrance, thus violating the aforementioned 1954 Supreme Court ruling, as well as the resulting federally mandated integration. Three days later, President Eisenhower got involved, sending Faubus a telegram that read in part: "The only assurance I can give you is that the Federal Constitution will be upheld by me by every legal means at my command." That, coupled with pressure from former Arkansas governor Sid McMath (whom Faubus had worked for earlier in his political career), persuaded Faubus to meet with Eisenhower on September 14. That conclave was sufficiently productive so as to convince Faubus to end his obstruction of federal law and on September 21, the National Guard was told to stand down. Two days later, however, Eisenhower was the recipient of a telegram, this time from Little Rock mayor Woodrow Mann, stating that the situation at Central High School was far from resolved. A mob had formed, which local police were attempting to control, and the newly enrolled "colored" students were sent home for their safety. Mann was convinced that the chief agitator was an associate of Faubus. In response, Eisenhower federalized the Arkansas National Guard and ordered them to return to their armories, effectively removing them from Faubus' control. He then sent the 101st Airborne Division of the US Army to enforce the court order and keep the peace. In retaliation, Faubus shut down Little Rock high schools for the 1958–1959 school year. This is often referred to in Little Rock lore as "The Lost Year".[7]

---

[7] Orval Faubus. (2024, October 5). In Wikipedia. https://en.wikipedia.org/wiki/Orval_Faubus

Given these events, how was Faubus able to get reelected multiple times? Faubus, ever the shrewd politician, campaigned as a populist and was able to convince many voters of the "us versus them" mentality. Arkansas' citizens saw Faubus as a crusader for states' rights and were wary of an overly powerful federal government that could mandate policies they were opposed to. His popularity did wane over the years, and he chose not to run for a seventh term. Interestingly enough, his views changed over time, and he actually supported Jesse Jackson during his 1984 and 1988 presidential runs! That said, the Faubus name will be forever linked to what Sims has dubbed the "Little Rock Shock," which he addresses in a follow-up soliloquy, along with the ineffectiveness of American Christian missionaries abroad. But it is his assessment of his family's current situation (and so many other families like the Sims) that is truly alarming.

~~~~~~

314 South Illinois Street
South Bend, Indiana
May 10, 1961

Dear Friends,

As always, for now, and forever more, your acquaintance and unfaltering friendship is uppermost in our minds. Our hearts rejoice at the knowledge of knowing our letter exchange and acquaintance has served to maintain a bond of thoughtfulness, love, and friendship on the part of you folks. Again, we say it is our desire for you to know that we pray nothing will ever be able to destroy this bond between our two families. Our family always looks forward to and anxiously awaits the arrival of your letters. We especially enjoy you sharing with us the various greetings and gifts and your thoughtfulness and concern about community, state and world well-being, for it gives us the opportunity to exchange ideas as to what is best for mankind and what must be done if we are to survive.

Recalling your letter reference about Dr. Lowell Gess, stating the difficulties missionaries abroad face in trying to practice Christian love in foreign missionaries due to our country's racial policies, I feel obligated and compelled to comment about it.

Recently, I recall reading a news item about Nigeria advising missionaries to return to their homeland, stating Christian brotherhood was not being practiced in America. Indeed, this is the obvious reason why Africans question the sincerity and intention of foreign missionaries in their countries.

However, I recall a sermon of a minister whose tilt was "Out of all bad things, some goodness must follow." He stated at that time that the conduct and action on the part of the racist of Little Rock - Governor Faubus - served to enlighten the world about deep-seated convictions instilled in people ever since slavery was abolished. The "Little Rock Shock" has forced this nation to be determined that this doesn't make a repeat performance, and in his opinion, this was the goodness of the incident.

I must say our people face an even greater danger than Little Rock. Presently, our people are facing actual starvation here in my state. We have a reputation for being an anti-welfare state. Without going into detail, our people are being cut off from relief, some with only $36.00 of unemployment to exist on, others with nothing. If somehow your church society could contact members of your faith in our state and prevail upon them to investigate relief conditions, this would certainly be a God-sent prayer answered. Believe me when I say men, women, and children by the thousands are going hungry and raggedy in our state today. Please forgive me for dwelling so long on the matter; however, I feel that human suffering in our wealthy land is so unnecessary and ungodly. I'm certain it may seem strange to you that I appeal to people in a state other than my own. If only time and space would permit me to explain the hardships, difficulties, and disappointment we have faced in trying to obtain aid to relieve the suffering of working people who are unemployed. I must confess to you that I have lost faith in some religious local organizations and people for whom I previously held in the highest esteem because of their seemingly unconcerned complacency, while local people go begging private charities for the bare necessities of life. Presently, life for some 1500 families in our city is almost unbearable. We will explain in detail later in other correspondence. If we are able to secure employment on the farms in Michigan, beginning about June 15, it is our desire and intention to visit with you between July 1st and 15th.

As always, our possibilities of earning a few cents are so uncertain that we dare not say anything other than we hope and pray we will be able to keep our word during these difficult times. Please convey our best wishes to your minister and the people of your community. Tell them we pray for the day that news of our community can be cheerful and not distressing, as it presently is.

The children send their love and best wishes to each of you. It is extremely embarrassing to ask you, but I feel I must eventually. I either forwarded the letter containing your birth dates to NBC or misplaced it. The only date we remember was your wedding anniversary: Dec. 24. Will you kindly forward this information to us in your next letter? We want so much to be able to share alike the thoughtfulness you have shared so much with our family.

With undying faith, love, and Christian devotion, we remain yours,

David & Ruby Sims and Family

P.S. We thought we would share this poem with you in the hope of furthering our understanding and friendship. Ruby plans to recite it in church on Mother's Day.

Regarding the aforementioned poem, it was not in the scrapbook nor the envelope containing the letter. Did Ruby compose it? If not, who did, and what was its title? The following theory has merit.

In a subsequent letter, Mr. Sims speaks of a poem entitled "The Negro Mother." It will be addressed further in Chapter 20. Its content would seem to be ideal for such an occasion. A simple Google search of the title will bring up a copy if the reader is interested in these venerable verses.

May 24, 1961
314 South Ill. St.
South Bend, Ind.

Dear Friends,

How are all of you? Fine, I hope.

Avard, the smallest boy in the family, has the mumps. He will be over it in a few days, we hope.

We are hoping to make it to Minnesota to visit all of you. All of us wanted to thank all of you for the food you sent us. I am writing a story. I will send you a copy when I finish. I haven't got a name for my story. When I send you a copy, you may name it for me.

I guess I'd better be closing now. Love from all of us.

Yours Sincerely,
Carla & Sims Family

I am hoping to get my book published. Tell me if you like my story.

~~~~~~

That last line in italics was scribbled on the back of the envelope containing Carla Diane's second letter to the Davids. Whether or not that story was ever written remains a mystery, as, when queried, Carla mentioned having no memory of the story or of writing a book. She suggested it was likely a reference to something her father was working on, but the handwriting in the letter and on the envelope are a match.

~~~~~~

R. R. #3 Box 100
Spring Valley, Minn.
May 25, 1961

Dear Friends,

First of all, let us thank you for the perfectly beautiful Mother's Day card you sent me. I can't tell you how much it is appreciated. The verse is beautiful, and we do enjoy it every day as we look at it in its place on top of the TV set.

Last Friday, we had to go to Iowa for seed beans that Sharkey bought from his brother. He will be planting them now just as quickly as he can get the ground prepared. We had such a pleasant surprise awaiting us there. Sharkey's brother John and his wife Neva have taken a darling 12-year-old Indian girl into their Christian home for the summer months. She is a little girl whose parents have abandoned her to a mission school in Nebraska. The school has many children in the same situation and is most anxious to have these children have the experience of family living during the summertime. We had such a good fellowship together that day, and when you folks come this summer, they want to come here and visit, so perhaps you will meet her, too. We mentioned that if we are all able to visit together, we shall have the beginnings of a miniature United Nations. It is wonderful how Christian love can bind men, women, and children of all races into a great brotherhood.

Your last letter, which concerned the plight of 1500 unemployed families in South Bend, has caused us great concern. We are in complete accord with your opinion that in a land such as ours, one who is industrious, capable, and willing to work should not have to suffer such hardship.

Pres. Kennedy has seemed quite concerned with this problem. We wondered if you are able to get Federal Aid through the surplus food commodities?

Since the new outbreak of violence in the South, it seems that our impending visit together has become more urgent than ever. World politics in the African and Asian countries are being decided in the light of the terrible things that are happening. We just must do something to show that there is some brotherhood of man to man in this country. Rev. Utzman is hoping your visit can be the first week of July as he will be here then, also.

The Minneapolis paper has a reporter who has called Rev. Utzman several times, wanting to know when our visit will be. I know when they come and witness the high regard, love and esteem we hold for each other, there can only come the kind of a story that will counteract some of the bad publicity that appears every day in the papers and that the enemies of our country use against us so forcibly.

Thank you so much for the enclosed clippings. I'm sure, Ruby, that when you read it in church on Mother's Day, it was a real blessing to all who heard it. In the future, we would so love to worship with you in your church some Sunday.

Please let us know the news about your coming and we will send the money for your trip and traveling expenses right away. Would you feel that $50.00 would enable you to have a safe journey here? Or perhaps the condition of your car would make it necessary for a larger amount to be sent. Please let us know what your feelings are about this.

To answer your inquiry about our birthdays:

Sharkey's is Dec. 24, 1917
Roselyn May 26, 1930
Joyce Aug. 25, 1956
Gregory Aug. 28, 1958

We hope the small love gift of food that we sent you reached you without too much damage in shipment.

We shall be waiting for further news from you soon.

Love from us all,
The Davids - Sharkey, Roselyn, Joyce, & Gregory

~~~~~~

314 South Ill. Street
South Bend, Indiana
June 1, 1961

Mr. and Mrs. Davids,

Dear Friends, the food parcels arrived undamaged and they were a welcome sight as it was needed by us since we are being forced to live on $36.00 per week by the overseer of the poor, among other things. However, my intent in appealing for your aid was more of a political nature. In our city, a person without means of support is given aid by the overseer of the poor. The law states the amount of food allowed should be adequate enough to maintain families in decent, healthy condition. The problem that I face, along with others, is that this section of the statute has been flagrantly violated by the overseer of the poor. Reliefers are allowed less than 12 cents per meal per person. This allowance is regulated by the township trustee who is the overseer of the poor. It's entirely up to him to raise or lower the amount allowed for families' food budgets.

Now, our people make up the majority on relief because we are usually the first to be laid off our jobs and are usually the last ones to be hired on the job, as seniority rules.

Reliefers are given a two-week food supply and are forced to do without or appeal to a private agency for the rest of the month. I hope it isn't too difficult for you to understand what I'm saying.

You recall my saying before my loss of confidence in people I previously held in high esteem? Well, the following organizations are well aware of the reliefers' plight, and to my knowledge and dismay, they have shown no outward concern about the community's plight. The Urban League has no part of relief in their program. Locally, the NAACP hasn't aided us legally, as the local chapter feels our civil rights haven't been violated. They remain silent while children go hungry. The industrial union council has endorsed the "Work for Relief Program" in our area where reliefer works for food received. This work for relief would be okay if they would supply all of our basic needs, but they don't. The union is also aware of the fact that reliefers only get one-half of what is necessary for the maintenance of life. Even though our area has been declared a distressed area, running higher than any other area in the country in unemployment, the union remains silent while former members are being denied adequate food as provided for by state law. And last, but not least, the St. Joseph Council of churches has shown no concern or publicly displayed any interest in attempting to get any increase in our diet allowance, even though we appeal constantly to their private charities for food supplements. It appears as though all civic, social, religious, labor, and other organizations in our area would rather leave things as they are rather than change them. The only reason given is that if reliefers are given an adequate diet, as the law provides for, reliefers would be content to never seek work as no job would be necessary because their basic needs of food, rent, shelter, etc., are being provided for through public assistance.

Therefore, they aren't too interested in fighting for a diet increase because it may tend to make reliefers lazy. The real reason they have no desire to aid our plight is because relief is paid for through property taxes in our area. If the inadequate diet is increased to the standard as provided for by law, property taxes probably will be increased again, and we have a very high rate as it is. Believe me when I say this is the real reason why they remain silent while people go hungry in our state. The only way a reliefer can get a diet increase presently is that it has to be recommended by a member of the medical profession. This only happens when one of our children, or an adult body, is so weakened that s/he can no longer resist diseases such as anemia, hepatitis, or some other dreadful disease.

Most of our people are helpless in their plight because they lack educational abilities to conduct, or rather compete with the people who they look to for aid while in distress. The Negro Ministry is completely inactive. They have no part in relief matters. Only one white Catholic priest, Father Thilman, has been able to aid reliefers when they meet with outright denial by the overseer of the poor. It's a result of his giving time and aid; so many of our people in distress went to him for advice until he had to stop upon doctor's orders. Otherwise, he would have had a breakdown. Our ministers seem to be content with these conditions. Their attitude is this is a political, rather than a religious, matter even though their members are without life's necessities. Inasmuch as anyone knows that the baby's first line of defense is an adequate diet, coupled with the fact that a reliefer must sign a powers affidavit declaring he has no means of earning a living, I feel that the church should take the lead in the fight to condemn "the existence diet theory" (just enough to keep a person on the borderline of starvation) as accepted and practiced in our community. To my knowledge, to date, the church has not openly or secretly concerned itself, even though they have been invited into reliefer's homes, the stores where they grade, etc. This "Conspiracy of Silence" on the part of that section of society, who is able

and should be willing to furnish the leadership
necessary to eliminate this evil condition, means
slow death for the masses through starvation. You
may recall a disease that was rampant among our
people during the other depression known as
pellagra, a disease caused by a diet deficiency. If
unemployment remains high, this condition will
exist again. These are a few of the reasons why I
say we face a greater danger than the passive
resistance fight for equality, and it would be a
blessing for some Christian organizations, such as
your missionary society, to investigate the problem
of religious focus. This is needed more than
anything else in our town today. I'm enclosing a
few items that will further your understanding as
to what I've attempted to do at community, state
and national levels. Government surplus we receive
consists of rice, beans, cornmeal, flour, lard, and
powdered milk. Recently, they added oatmeal,
powdered eggs, butterfat, and peanut butter. Please
note that most items listed consist of starches.
Reliefers are interested in a well-balanced diet:
some parts of the seven basic foods. Daily, we feel
that so long as the federal government is going to
aid us, they should at least see to it we get a
balanced diet out of whatever is given by them.
This is not being done here in our area. This is
just one of the many problems we are faced with
that no one here in leadership seems to be concerned
about. This is what distresses me so much.

About our trip: you recall me saying it was our intention to pick fruit in Michigan, usually around June 15, as strawberries are ready for harvest. Well, this year, we had a killer frost, so the crops are ruined (the early ones, that is). We were counting on earning the necessary vacation money there.

You were entirely correct when you said the condition of our car was such that it would require more than $50.00 to journey to your home. The engine went bad in our station wagon in December. I've been informed by a mechanic that it would take a minimum of one hundred dollars (labor, parts, etc.) to repair the engine since a bearing went bad and scored the crankshaft, and it has to be reground. It was our intent, hope, and desire to earn this money on the farms in Michigan. I'm certain you now realize why we say everything is so uncertain until we dare not say for certain when or what we will be able to do.

Give our best regards to Rev. Utzman and all, and tell him, do not hesitate or delay his vacation on our account for the way life presently exists for us. Only heaven knows when and if we will ever be able to journey to your community.

Kindly say hello to your grandmother for us. We are very eager to hear from her. We are taking it for granted that your immediate family is well in health. We still feel that someday, somehow, we shall come to your home. Again, let us thank you very much for the gifts, love, and kindness you have shown our family. Ruby and all the children – and, of course, myself – send our very best wishes. Even though it's a little late, we wish you many more happy birthdays and the best in health and spirit for you and yours.

With all our love,
David and Ruby, Sims and the Children

~~~~~~

R. R. #3 Box 100
Spring Valley, Minn.
June 4, 1961

Dear David, Ruby & children,

We received your letter yesterday and we took it immediately to Rev. Utzman. After quite a lengthy discussion, we came to three conclusions.

Rev. Utzman knows our Evangelical United Brethren pastor in South Bend and has written a letter to him telling him of our relationship and of the plight of the 1500 families in your area.

He is asking this man to get in contact with you and find out first-hand about the problem. His name is Rev. Robert Haskins. We're hoping that he is the kind of man we believe him to be so that he will be able to aid you in some way. At least he should know of the problem in the city he now serves as pastor.

Rev. Utzman is writing the mayor of your city, telling him that the situation is such, that attention is being forced on South Bend from points as far away as Minnesota, and are asking him to do something constructive to aid all his people.

Sometimes, when things look the very darkest, a ray of light suddenly shines through, and we think we have figured out a way to make it possible for you to come here this summer. If you will come, we will come after you. We shall leave here sometime during the day of June 30 (Friday) and be at your home the morning of Sat. July 1. There are so many people who are interested in making this visit possible that we shall come in two cars — our car and the car of another couple who are friends of ours.

We feel that we want to keep faith with you. You are doing so much for your people and the cause of justice; we want to encourage you in every way we know how. Please keep the $50.00 that Rev. Utzman sent you for trip expenses like meals, etc. on the way here and back again. Two more cars will be made available to make the journey back to your home on Mon. or Tues. July 10 or 11. This would make it possible for you to spend two Sundays of fellowship with us.

We feel that this time together will be so very profitable for so many, and our earnest prayer is that you will feel you can say "yes" and come.

Our love to you as Christian brothers – as always –
The Davids

PS: Please let us know as soon as possible.

~~~~~~

314 South Illinois Street
South Bend 19, Indiana
June 10, 1961

Mr. and Mrs. Davids,

Dearest friends, we realized you were anxious to receive a reply about our decision. We hesitated to answer only because we dare not impose such travel hardship and expense upon your generosity.

Ruby's uncle was able to secure an engine for our car for $25.00. The seller claimed the motor to be in good condition. A mechanic promised to install the engine beginning Monday week. So, we are hoping to be able to make the trip in our car. If we see where it can't be possible to get ours in good running condition so we can come, we will inform you by the 25th of June, so you will have ample time to come after us if this is agreeable with and acceptable to you folks.

It will not be possible for us to leave until July 3, 1961 because our only income is the $36.00 unemployment check, which I must be here to sign for cash on Monday of every week. This would leave us July 4, 5, 6, 7, 8, 9 and only one Sunday with you. I'm sure you understand that we simply

115

need this money desperately.

We know you folks are probably tired of hearing the words "our hearts leaped for joy"; however, we find it difficult to find words to better describe to you our feelings when we say we are honored to be associated with folks such as yourselves.

You folks appear to be blessed with mankind's greatest gift – the ability to give of yourselves to others unselfishly – not with pity or pride, but with humility and sacrifice. This is the greatest gift God has bestowed upon mankind. In our minds, these qualities are essential and necessary for the salvation of the world and needed by nations to stabilize world peace.

We neglected to write to your minister, Rev. Utzman, after receiving your letter. And because he did not enclose a box number or address, we feared he may not have received our reply. We are enclosing his letter. Would you be so kind as to see that he receives it and express our regret for the delay?

We have been the receivers of so much kindness from you folks, we hardly know how to express our gratitude. It is our desire to give rather than be the receiver all the time. We want to be able to bring joy to others as others have brought joy to us, especially you folks.

I managed to struggle through school with a couple of B's and C's. It was extremely difficult to study when faced with domestic hardships, but I made it, and we are so happy.

Ruby, the children, and myself eagerly and anxiously await the coming visit. We will be glad to make the journey. We want to hear from you soon.

Sincerely with all our love,
David & Ruby Sims and Children

~~~~~~

Regarding the letters written by Rev. Utzman, if positive measures were taken to better the quality of life for those 1500 struggling households, no evidence could be found. That said, armed with a vehicle sporting a working engine and the $50 sent to cover travel expenses, the Sims family seems poised to depart on July 3rd, barring any other setbacks.

~~~~~~

R. R. 3 Box 100
Spring Valley, Minn.
June 22, 1961

Dear Friends,

We are so happy about your decision to come here for your trip. We anticipate some days of wonderful Christian fellowship together.

Since we shall be visiting very soon, I shall not make this a lengthy letter, but we want to make sure that you have the directions to our home.

I suppose we may expect you late Monday night, July 3, so we shall leave our yard light on as a sort of landmark for you. We do wish you a safe, happy drive, and our prayers go with you each mile of the way.

If anywhere along the way you should have any difficulties, please call us collect. Our phone number is Racine, Minn. 2488.

Racine is a very tiny town. Only one street (main street) comes off of Highway 63 into the town. It turns off east right by a large grain elevator. This main street continues right along east for 2 miles into the country, then ½ mile north, then 2 ½ miles east to our home. After you have left Highway 63, the road becomes a black top; then on the ½ mile north, it becomes gravel. The road past our home is gravel.

I hope I haven't confused you with these last details. Goodbye for now, and I hope to see you soon.

Our love,
Sharkey, Roselyn, Joyce & Gregory

~~~~~~

After two years of correspondence, planning, and praying, everything seems to be falling into place for the Sims family to finally make the South Bend to Spring Valley sojourn a reality.

R. R. #3 Box 100
Spring Valley, Minn.
July 2, 1961

Mr. Peter Lassally
Producer Image Series
N.B.C. Inc.
RCA Bldg. 30 Rockefeller Plaza
New York 20, New York

Dear Mr. Lassally,

In 1959, we became acquainted with the David Sims family of South Bend, Indiana, after hearing them on your Image Minority Series (Radio).

After many letters of friendship and much planning, it has at last become possible for them to visit us July 3 – 8.

A reporter from a Minneapolis paper wanted to do a story on our visit, and then we remembered that Bob Considine had expressed the desire to cover this story. This is why we thought we had better drop you a line to let you know of our visit this week.

Our church and community have gone all out to help us make this interracial visit possible, so we are looking forward to a very happy and interesting week. Thank you for your part in this.

Sincerely,
Mr. & Mrs. Marienus Davids

Since Mrs. Davids agreed to keep both Lassally and Considine in the loop regarding the progress on fulfilling her original invitation to the Sims, she felt compelled to write this letter, the last piece of correspondence prior to the Sims' anticipated arrival. When Roselyn made a promise, she kept it.

Chapter 10: It's Been Just Like Christmas

As there was now no need to go get them, Roselyn anxiously awaited the arrival of her passionate pen pal and his trepidatious travelers, as did Sharkey, Joyce, and Gregory. The Sims departed South Bend sometime in the afternoon of July 3rd, shortly after David signed for his unemployment check. The journey from northern Indiana to southeastern Minnesota, with minimal stops and no car trouble, would be a good ten hours – maybe more – getting them to their destination late that evening or early the next morning.

Eventide had long since come and gone in the Sumner Center area, replaced by the ebony of a murky, starless night. Yard lights of surrounding acreages dotted the darkness like eerie, glowing spheres. The Davids' porch light had been on for many hours, providing a beacon of sorts for all who would take refuge at this quaint farmhouse. A vestige of illumination, courtesy of the moon, peaked through the clouds just as a pair of headlights appeared in the distance, growing ever larger and brighter as they approached. Shortly, an older model blue and white Dodge slowed its pace, turning off the dusty gravel road and onto the dirt driveway of the Davids' family homestead.

As it came to a stop, the Davids quartet, having waited up to give these weary road warriors a royal welcome, scooted out the back door and onto the porch, all smiles, eager to greet their new house guests. The porch light provided just enough brightness to behold a scene reminiscent of the unloading of a Volkswagen Beetle after a people-stuffing contest. The car doors opened, and the Sims family members

– all eleven of them, plus their German Shepherd, Midnight – exited, one after another. Little Joyce, mouth agape, asked her mother how eleven people could fit in one car. Roselyn tilted her head downward and gave Joyce what was to become known among the Davids children as "the look." Even at five years old, precocious Joyce was well aware of what that ominous leer meant. With a devilish grin, she buttoned her lip and returned her gaze to the newly arrived visitors, who were now all out of the vehicle. As the two families descended upon each other, hugs and handshakes abounded, reminiscent of their meeting in South Bend one year previous. David Sims would later be quoted as saying, "They met us with open arms, love, and kindness." [8]

Such pleasantries, however delightful, could not mitigate the exhaustion of a tiresome trek, so after a snack and a bit of "catching up", the Sims, adult and child alike, were ready to hit the sack. Roselyn had prepared the upstairs bedrooms for them, and they retired in short order, knowing the active participation in the bevy of activities the Fourth of July was sure to bring would require a good night's sleep. Where the Davids' kin laid their heads that night is uncertain. There were no downstairs bedrooms at the time (a master was added to the main floor years later) and those upstairs had limited privacy. The sofa for Sharkey? Perhaps a reclining chair for Roselyn? Maybe blankets overlaying the living room rug for Joyce and Greg? 'Tis mere conjecture.

---

[8] "Minnesotans Show Kindness to Negro Family." Seattle Post-Intelligencer, July 10, 1961.

The eldest Sims daughter, Charlotte, who was 13 at the time, recollects that everyone arose well-rested the next morning and, thanks to the family matriarchs, were treated to a hearty breakfast of eggs, toast, and bacon. She also recalls Sim's and David's siblings playing together shortly thereafter, with Joyce leading the way in the exploration of the farm and interaction with the animals. It was obvious that for them, race was not a barrier. Mrs. Davids would later recount, "The children have never mentioned color. Our children are much too young to be prejudiced, and they have never been taught prejudice." She added, after observing the children romp and frolic with one another, that "they just love each other now."[9]

The Sims visit becoming a reality required a community effort. Of the $50 sent to the Sims for travel expenses, half was donated directly by church members who wanted to see this through.[10] Some hosted the Sims for a meal or even an overnight; others brought donations of food and/or clothing. Most had never before met persons of color, but that did not impede their generosity or neighborliness. Many swung by the farm to revel in the Independence Day festivities. Moreover, relatives from Iowa drove up, as was their custom on the Fourth of July. Including the hosts and their guests of honor, 38 people would take part in the celebration at the residence of Roselyn and Sharkey. As they gathered for the main meal of the day, the picnic table outside seated eighteen children and included a Native American girl who was being sponsored for the summer by Sharkey's brother, John, as

---

[9] Pennington, David. "Sumner Center White Family, South Bend Negroes Try Human Relations Experiment." Rochester Post-Bulletin, July 7, 1961.
[10] Negro Family Taken In And Everyone Is Happy." Minneapolis Star, (n.d.)

well as his three girls, the Sims, and kids from neighboring farms.

The food for that meal, by the way, was donated. "The Interdenominational Birthday Club, to which Mrs. Davids belongs, had flooded the home with food, 'more than we can hope to eat up,' she said proudly."[11]

Club members were diligent about bringing at least one meal's worth of food to the Davids' residence every day during the Sims' stay. "It's been just like Christmas," added Roselyn, no doubt grinning ear to ear.

Wednesday brought the largest influx of visitors of any day that week and included 44 friends and neighbors from the Sumner Center area, as well as nearby towns. Many of the women were members of the church Mission Society, who "came to visit, bringing clothing and canned food that the Sims will take home with them when they leave Monday morning. What the Sims can't use, they will distribute to their friends in South Bend, many of whom are also unemployed."[12]

That evening, two of the Sims girls – Charlotte and Carla Diane – were invited to and attended a nearby 4-H meeting. The event's activities had a lasting effect on Carla Diane, who recounts, "I do remember going to the 4-H fair. That also got me involved in the 4-H fairs in Indiana."

---

[11] Pennington, David. "Sumner Center White Family, South Bend Negroes Try Human Relations Experiment." Rochester Post-Bulletin, July 7, 1961.
[12] Ibid.

Of course, reporters came out to the farm, hoping to be the first ones to get the scoop on how this interracial experiment was progressing. Charlotte recalls meeting them, though she could not be certain of the reporter's questions or her responses to them. Her recollection leaned toward Tuesday, July 4th, a distinct possibility since there were likely multiple occurrences. But evidence in the way of a ledger entry suggests Thursday, July 6th. You see, Roselyn kept a guest book during this time and asked visitors to sign it. While not everyone did, two names of import show up on this date, both with the Rochester Post-Bulletin: Charles B. Hale and David Pennington. The latter is quoted in an earlier chapter and is the author of some of the articles from the Post-Bulletin that appear in Mrs. Davids' scrapbook. Much of the information in this chapter is gleaned from those accounts.

Interviews conducted by the aforementioned Hale and Pennington occupied much of Thursday morning and perhaps later that evening. Both families were invited that afternoon over to the Lawrence Bussman farm, just up the road from the Davids. Pennington would go on to write that "the Bussmans, who are Catholic, were so impressed with the Sims, who are Baptist, that they asked them if they knew of another Negro family in South Bend that they could invite up to their home next year."[13]

Later that evening, the elder Sims boys were invited to attend a baseball game and did so with some of the lads their age from neighboring farms.

---

[13] Pennington, David. "Sumner Center White Family, South Bend Negroes Try Human Relations Experiment." Rochester Post-Bulletin, July 7, 1961.

Friday brought more excitement – not all of it good – as some of the Sims children returned to the Bussmans early that morning to help them milk their cows. Later that day, many went swimming at the Spring Valley public pool. As there were no Negro families living in Spring Valley at the time, the hospitality shown to the visitors was sorely lacking compared to that of the Sumner residents. There were whispers and furled brows aplenty, sometimes accompanied by pointing and a shouted racial epithet. Carla Diane recalls discussing this later with her mother. Ruby, in typical super-mom fashion, soothed her child's hurt feelings and convinced her that everything would be okay. As a fitting climax to an otherwise convivial day, both families were dinner guests of Rev. and Mrs. Utzman and enjoyed a lovely evening of food and Christian fellowship.

The weekend ushered in the two busiest days of the entire stay. Saturday was all about sight-seeing. A dear friend of the family, Donald Miller, acted as tour guide in showing the families around Rochester. They visited the IBM plant where he was employed at the time, the Mayo Clinic, and, having his pilot's license, even provided the Sims with their very first airplane ride... well, the two oldest boys, anyway. The Rochester romp came to a close with a duck feeding at Silver Lake (each Sims child was given an ear of corn before leaving the farm). The evening culminated in dinner at the neighboring farm of beloved friends Mr. and Mrs. Ivan Snyder, who were hosting two Native American boys for the summer. Also in attendance that night were the Harold Kings, who contributed to the international flavor of the occasion via the two 13-year-old Japanese young ladies they were sponsoring at the time.[14] All told, 17 children from four different races played on the teeter-totter, engaged in croquet, and rode horses, all without the slightest inkling of the example they were setting for all who would read about this seminal affair. The Sims and Davids – in fact, the entire Sumner community – embodied the teachings of Martin Luther King, Jr. two years before the delivery of his iconic "I Have a Dream" speech.

Sunday was a day of worship for these two devoutly Christian families, and this day would be no exception. With the Sims as honored guests, the small, country Evangelical United Brethren church was packed. Rev. Utzman counted 160-plus people – the largest crowd to ever attend a service during his tenure there. Music was provided by the entire Sims family, sans 18-month baby Belinda, as they regaled the appreciative crowd with Negro spirituals and other scripture-based hymns.[15] Following the uplifting service, most of the congregation proceeded on to a public park in Spring Valley, where they continued celebrating by way of a potluck picnic for the ages. They were joined by neighbors and friends of all different faiths and beliefs, but they all shared a common goal: to give the Sims family the time of their lives and to let them know that while prejudice and racism may be the soup du jour in some parts of the country, those who call this quaint Minnesota township home don't order from that menu.

---

[14] "White Couple Hosts Negro Family Here." Spring Valley Tribune, Vol. 81, No. 26, July 13, 1961.
[15] Pennington, David. "Sumner Center White Family, South Bend Negroes Try Human Relations Experiment." Rochester Post-Bulletin, July 7, 1961.

Alas, Monday morning arrived, and it was time for the Sims and Davids to say their goodbyes. It was bittersweet for both families, but especially so for the Sims. After a wonderful week of food and fellowship, David, Ruby, and the children had to leave their new-found friends and return to South Bend, where they faced enormous uncertainties. But they would not be departing the farm empty-handed. Donations of food and clothing were a daily occurrence throughout the week, so much so that there was no room in their vehicle for such generosities. A U-Haul trailer had to be rented to haul the nearly 200 jars and cans of food, not to mention the dresses, shirts, pants, shoes, and other articles of clothing given to them so graciously by the Sumner patrons. The $20 rental fee was paid for by the church's Youth Fellowship group, which had recently earned money for missionary projects.[16] But members of the Sims family would leave the Davids' farm with far more than provisions; each harbored memories of time spent with marvelous people who cared not a whit about skin color, as well as activities never before experienced. Carla Diane recalls one such exploit. "I got to spend the night alone with a girl named Emilie (Snyder) and her family, who lived close to the farm. I shared with my mom that I was a little uncomfortable going to their home. Mom said that they were good Christians and friends to the Davids and everything would be fine staying all night with Emilie and her family. I remember getting up the next morning and going downstairs to a really nice breakfast and Emilie and her parents being very kind to me. I had a wonderful time sleeping over at

---

[16] "A Freedom Ride with a Different Ending." The Minnesota Conference News Review, August 1961, Vol. 13, p. 4.

Emilie's home."

But did the Sims have to return to South Bend? More than one source proffers the notion (confirmed by Charlotte) that the Sims were offered a fully-furnished house in the Spring Valley area (by whom or what entity is not known) and that Mr. Sims would be provided employment[17] (the nature of which was not specified). While the tempting proposal was considered, the proud patriarch, citing safety concerns, as well as a sense of duty to his South Bend compatriots, ultimately decided to return his family to their Indiana home despite objections from the children. "The hospitality of this community has been wonderful," the faithful father of nine explained. "We've never experienced anything like it. The children have had the time of their lives and don't want to go home."[18]

Ruby Sims, in a postcard sent to a neighbor earlier in the week, echoed those sentiments. "Everyone is doing fine. We can't wait until we get back home so we can talk about all of the wonderful things that are happening to us. The people here are wonderful."[19]

---

[17] "Negro Family Praises Visit." South Bend Tribune, July 10, 1961, p. 21.
[18] "Farm Couple Host to Negro Family." South Bend Tribune, July 8, 1961.
[19] Ibid.

Chapter 11: Photos, Notes, and Quotes

The only reporters documented in Mrs. Davids' guest book to have visited the farm are the aforementioned gentlemen from the *Rochester Post-Bulletin*. However, there were undoubtedly others. Roselyn mentions in a previous letter that a Minneapolis newspaper reporter was interested in interviewing both families and most likely did. As word spread, accounts of the historic visit began appearing in articles published in magazines and newspapers throughout the country and many were clipped and pasted into Roselyn's scrapbook. Attempts were made to contact all publications; some granted permission for their content to be utilized in this book; others ceased circulation long ago and did not respond to inquiries. The footnotes thus far reveal that the *Rochester Post-Bulletin* is the most commonly quoted source, but invaluable information was also provided by the *South Bend Tribune* and *Spring Valley Tribune*, as well as the *Church of the Brethren Gospel Messenger* and *The Minnesota Conference E.U.B. Church News Review*. Stories from the latter two are reprinted here. Roselyn's scrapbook also contains write-ups from the *Denver Post*, the *Ponca City News*, and the *Chicago Tribune*, plus a handful of unsourced articles.

The Davids also received from Jet Magazine a complimentary copy of the Aug. 10, 1961 edition, which contains a feature highlighting the historic affair, complete with farm photos. While it cannot be reprinted here, it can be read online. Simply google "archived Jet Magazine issues" and click on <u>The Online Books Page</u> entry. Then click the link included in the sentence "1951-2008: Google Books has most of the print run of this magazine." From there, you can navigate to this edition.

MINNESOTA CONFERENCE NEWS REVI

A FREEDOM RIDE WITH A DIFFERENT ENDING

Mr. and Mrs. Marienus Davids, Mr. and Mrs. David Sims, Harold and David Jr. chat at an all-church picnic.

(Courtesy of Austin Herald)

A thrilling experience in racial brotherhood took place in the Sumner Center community recently. On July 4, Mr. and Mrs. David Sims and their nine children arrived to spend a week with the Marienus Davids, members of the Sumner Center congregation. The Sims are Negroes from South Bend, Indiana.

It all began in the summer of 1959 when Mr. Sims was being interviewed on an NBC radio series entitled "Image Minorities." One of the questions he was asked was, "Have you ever been in the home of a white family?" When he answered "No," Mrs. Davids ran out to the barn where Marienus was milking. They talked it over, wrote NBC for the Sims' address, and began a fruitful correspondence.

The visit of the Sims family was actually planned for last summer, with the Sumner Center Council of Administration voting $25 to help with their traveling expenses. At that time, however, Mr. Sims was working as a lathe operator for Studebaker and did not feel he could leave his job. His unemployment this year made it possible for them to come.

About 100 members of the church and community visited them during their stay. Many had never met a Negro personally. The Birthday Club, an interdenominational group in the community, also brought in a meal each day. When the time came for the Sims to leave they had been given so many gifts of food and clothing that a U-haul trailer was needed to

Page Four

carry it all back. The Youth Fellowship, which had recently earned $171 for missionary projects at a "Slave Auction," voted to pay the $20 rental fee.

"This has been a wonderful experience," Rev. Don Utzman said. "It has been as thrilling for the people of our community as for the Sims'. In these days when racial strife is trumpeted throughout the land we need more experiences such as these which show that white can meet with black in a spirit of genuine friendship and understanding. The interest on the part of the press has also been most gratifying. Not that this was done for publicity, but if the publicity which has come from it can help turn some bitterness and prejudice into love and understanding, surely God will be working through it."

Mr. Davids is a member of the Board of Trustees at Sumner Center and Mrs. Davids directs the choir and is president of the WSWS. "We just wanted to have the chance to practice what we preach," she said. "I think it was one of Pearl Buck's books that originally inspired me to do something like this. There was a quotation in it that goes something like this, 'How can white men save the souls of the Negro for heaven when they won't let them in their own houses?'"

The Kiester EUB Men entertained the Rice Lake EUB Men at a steak fry June 28, with 44 men in attendance.

This write-up from the *Minnesota Conference News Review (August 1961 Volume 13)* is included in its entirety, as it contains quotes from Rev. Utzman and Mrs. Davids that are more impactful when read from their source. The insert is one of the higher-quality photos available, but the caption contains an error. Yes, it was taken at the all-church picnic that followed the church service on July 10th. However, Mr. Sims is actually David Jr., as his father was David Sr. The handsome young man wearing the cap is David III.

Negro Family Guests of Church Couple

►A Negro couple and their nine children spent a week's vacation at a farm in Minnesota because a church woman learned they had never been invited into a white home. David Sims, an unemployed lathe operator of South Bend, Ind., and his family were treated royally during their stay on the Marienus Davids farm.

Neighbors who did not invite the Sims family to dine with them brought food by the carful for their meals at the Davids home. "It was just like Christmas," Mrs. Davids said.

The Sims children went to a 4-H club meeting and to a baseball game with other youngsters in the area. On a Sunday morning, the Simses, who are Baptists, showed appreciation for the hospitality by singing at the service of the Sumner Center Evangelical United Brethren church.

Also present at the service and a community picnic that followed were two American Indian children and two Oriental youngsters, all from the Twin Cities, who were guests of other members of the EUB congregation in the program of interracial visits sponsored by the Minnesota Council of Churches.

The idea of inviting the Sims family to their farm came to Mrs. Davids when she heard Mr. Sims

interviewed on a network radio program in June 1959. He said, in response to the question, that he had never been invited into a white family's home.

"I went to the barn and talked to my husband and he agreed the Sims family should be invited to our home," Mrs. Davids recalled. So she wrote to the president of the National Broadcasting Company in New York and got Mr. Sims' address. A long correspondence followed and last August Mr. and Mrs. Davids, on a visit to relatives in Illinois, got a chance to visit the Simses.

They were unable to come to Minnesota in 1959 when the invitation was extended because of lack of money. In August 1960, they were all set to come but Mr. Sims got a chance instead to work four days a week in a South Bend auto plant. This summer the invitation was renewed, and with the help of the church the trip finally materialized.

Mrs. Davids said she wanted to invite the Simses to see if she could practice what she believes about race relations. The experiment, she added, was "a howling success." — *Religious News Service.*

Mr. and Mrs. Marienus Davids, left, dish out food for Mr. and Mrs. David Sims, whom they entertained for a week with their nine children

AUGUST 19, 1961

This article appeared in the Aug. 19, 1961 Vol. 110 edition of the *Gospel Messenger*, a weekly publication by "The Church of the Brethren", who were eager to assist in the telling of this "fascinating" story. The photo caption mentions the sets of parents but omits the lovely little cherub in the foreground, who is Cheryl Sims. It was taken in the rustic dining room of the Davids' farmhouse, where many a scrumptious meal was shared with this godly couple.

As of the writing of this book, three of the nine Sims children have passed away: Avard (8/2009), Fredonya (10/2016), and Harold (4/2023). The surviving six siblings were encouraged to share their fondest memories of that eventful seven days. Carla Diane, whose recollections seem to be the most vivid, mused, "The food at Mrs. Roselyn and Mr. Sharkey's home was delicious and fresh. I am a foodie and really loved the food." She added, "I remember watching the cows going to their own stalls as Mr. Sharkey called them by name. I never knew at that age – eleven years – that cows had names."

Despite being the third oldest Sims child, Charlotte admits that her recollection of many of the activities of that fun-filled week is somewhat fuzzy. It was, after all, 63 years ago! But one thing that does stand out in her mind is a back-and-forth between her mom and Mrs. Davids regarding gardening.

"Roselyn was showing us around the farm. My mother spotted what Roselyn always assumed were weeds, and we knew them as mustard greens. My mother pulled them up, washed them, and they became part of our dinner that night!! They were delicious to Roselyn and she was so excited about a new nutritious food which could be added to her family's diet. The mustard greens are a vegetable that goes back to our Black people's ancestry when we had to scavenge food. So, we learned what was edible and it helped us to survive."

The above photo was likely taken at the Snyder farm during the Saturday shindig. The one below was probably snapped at the Sunday picnic in Spring Valley and is the only color photo in Roselyn's scrapbook. Note the absence of the David children and some of the Sims, which seems to be more than made up for with neighborhood kids.

Fredonya enjoys herself at the Spring Valley public swimming pool.

Baby Belinda gets an affectionate bear hug from Joyce's cousin, Wilma.

Group photo of both families, although, again, the site remains a mystery. It is definitely not the Davids farm. It could be at a neighbor's farm or, given the nature of the building window, a business in town. Also, note the automobile. Charlotte confirms this to be the very vehicle that transported all eleven family members – and their dog – to the farm and home again. Kudos to the entire Sims family for the tremendous fortitude and resiliency exhibited throughout this ambitious adventure.

Chapter 12: The Good, the Bad, and the Ugly

Whether it be from the reading of newspaper and magazine articles or simply by word of mouth, news of the Minnesota interracial experiment quickly traveled near and far, garnering a slew of reactions from supporters and detractors alike. The Davids received many letters, some expressing admiration and gratitude for the Christian love shone to the Sims. Others expressed their contempt for the Caucasian couple in ways that can best be summed up as "How dare you expose our white children to n*@@#^s."[20] The ignorance and animus on display are truly astounding and exemplify how divided the country was at that time regarding this issue. It is interesting to note that while all individuals who lauded Roselyn and Sharkey for their actions penned names to their letters, those who derided the Davids did not, with one lone exception. Some letters are excluded for extremely vile content, illegible cursive, or excessive details irrelevant to the subject. All others, pro and con, are included, minus the names and addresses (for privacy reasons), to give the reader some idea of what both families had to endure. Charlotte confirmed that the Sims received similar letters, predominantly critical – some were death threats – but their whereabouts are unknown and, as such, are not included here.

---

[20] "Minn. Whites Praised, Blamed for Having Negro House Guests." Jet Magazine, August 10, 1961.

July 4, 1961

Dear Madam,

Suppose you will get a few tart letters after your uncalled-for stunt. I have nothing against color or creed if they don't mix – but I have been on welfare duty for years, and I know that the greatest sin is when colored and white mix, also, Roman and Protestant religions. I have seen the mixed-up minds go down because the mixed ones do not know where they belong and damn both black and white. This city is burdened with troubles from the influx of these people with large families they cannot afford – it's a sin, and you must not have a girl of your own or son, one that was misled and ruined the rest of her and her young one's life.

I know the slimy politicians and the radicals promote this type of mix. If God wanted one type of people, he would have created such – but the Tower of Babel was destroyed because some reactionary tried to promote a universal language. The promoters of racial integration will destroy their purpose – by the stupid actions of black and white. Remember, the commies want internal discord.

Minn X – welfare worker

July 9, 1961

Dear Mrs. Davids,

I saw the grand write-up in the Minneapolis paper last night. It is so nice to know that at least your hopes were realized. From the account, I know the families are having a wonderful time and the community is pitching in, as you told us that day you knew they would.

I only wish others across the country could follow suit. I've just returned from a mission for Governor Anderson to check on the treatment "freedom riders" are being given in Mississippi. What a long way the people in Mississippi will have to come in the next few years.

Enclosed is the clipping from the paper. I'm sure you'd like an extra copy.

Sincerely,
G.B.

The "clipping from the paper" could be an article in the July 8 edition of the *Minneapolis Star* entitled "Spring Valley Couple Opens Home to Negro Family of Eleven." Although Roselyn's scrapbook features no such story, the previously cited "Negro Family Taken In And Everyone Is Happy" is a part of the collection, and its fold lines would allow for a perfect fit inside an envelope.

July 8, 1961
Mr. and Mrs. Marienus Davids
Spring Valley, Minn.

Dear friends in Christ,

Today, we read the article which appeared in the Minneapolis Star of your hospitality to the David Sims family. We want to commend you on your Christ-like example.

I am a missionary to Nigeria, West Africa. We are in Minneapolis with our daughter, who contracted polio in Nigeria and is receiving treatment here, but our home is only a few miles from South Bend, Ind.

As I read the article, I felt I should write and say how much I appreciate what you are doing. I feel we, as a church, have failed the colored people in America. We are happy for what our church is doing for the colored in other lands, and we need to be doing a lot more for them. But we have somehow failed to show Christ's love for those who live close to us. If we would show more love for them here, then our efforts of love on the other side of the ocean would show brighter. The news of America's segregation problem has traveled around the world, and it is hard to say I love you in Africa and neglect their people in our own land.

We do pray that the Lord will richly bless you for your expression of love to Him through doing it for others. Christ said, "And whosoever shall give you a cup of water in my name...he shall not lose his reward."

Your friends in Christ,
L.L.

~~~~~~

Sunday 7/9/61

My Dear Mr. & Mrs. Davids -

Just read about your guests from Indiana enjoying their vacation at your home.

Congratulations! And may God Bless You and Yours for the courage you had.

If only more people had the courage to do the things they believe in, this would be a much better place to live in. I'm very happy that your community did join with you in making your guests welcome.

I wonder what would happen in a large city (like Milwaukee) if someone invited Negroes to visit them.

May God Love You & Reward You.
R.V.A.

(P.S. I am white.)

July 10, 1961

Dear Mr. and Mrs. Davids:

I was truly thrilled to read of your recent
kindness to the David Sims family in Sunday's
edition of the Fargo Forum.

What a wonderful thing you have done. If only there
were more people who would extend similar
invitations.

God Bless you for your thoughtfulness and kindness.

Yours very truly,
C.F.

~~~~~~

July 11, 1961
Mrs. Marienus Davids
Spring Valley, Minn.

My dear Mrs. Davids,

I was quite interested in the news item in the
Minneapolis Star of July 8. Congratulations on your
kindness in giving this family a nice vacation.

I was also interested because I learned to know
Christ as my Savior in the Sumner Center Evangelical
Church in 1896. It was a new building at the time,
and Rev. Gaetz was the pastor. I can't recall the
name of the evangelist, but I can still see him in
my mind's eye. I have always looked back to that
little church as my spiritual birthplace...the name
just came to my mind: Rev. Zabel. I believe he was

the pastor when we moved back to Otter Tail County in the Spring of 1896.

I made a trip back there in '48 or '49, visited a cousin in Rochester, and they took us back to see the old schoolhouse and the church. I would like to have had at least a day, but there were several other places they wanted to take us, so we only had half a day.

I've been wondering where you folks live, in which direction, and how far from the church? Were your folks in the neighborhood at the time the church was built* and what their names were?

What I would like to know is where you folks live and if it is possible that I know your folks. I am soon 74 so I know you were not there at the time.

If you would be interested in answering my questions and telling me about yourselves and the church, I would appreciate it very much. Some of the happiest days of my life were spent down there, and I've been so thankful so many times that I found my Saviour at an early age. He has been a wonderful Saviour, Master, Leader, and Friend to me, and I have only one wish now: that each day I may live to please Him so that others can see Jesus in me. I'm enclosing a stamped envelope and am looking forward to hearing from you.

Sincerely,

Mrs. A.J.

* The Davids did not live in the area at that time. They bought the farm and moved to Minnesota from Iowa in February of 1957. Did Roselyn strike up a penpal relationship with the previous letter's author? Possibly, but there is no evidence in the way of further correspondence between the two.

~~~~~~

July 12, 1961

My dear Mrs. Davids & husband,

I read about your kindly act to the Sims family in our local paper, and I felt I wanted to drop you a note to tell you how much I admired your courage and unselfishness.

I wish there were more people in our wonderful country that would take time from their work to bring a little enjoyment to others.

Also, your whole community is to be honored for its part in the affair.

Sincerely yours,
J.H.

~~~~~~

July 12, 1961

Dear Mr. and Mrs. Davids,

I read about you in the paper. How nice you were to the colored family. If there were more people like you and your family and neighbors, there wouldn't be all this bloodshed. Sit-ins and picket lines would be unnecessary for the Negro to gain rights already guaranteed them.

I would so love to do as you have done. I guess I should explain why I can't. I am 29, an invalid in a wheelchair. I live with my family as I have no other place to live. I can't even care for myself much less help anyone else. I can bathe and feed myself with gadgets I have designed.

My family and I have had much disagreement on racial prejudice. We don't discuss it now. We realize we can't agree.

If there were more love and compassion and less hate, this would be a much better world. And maybe we could spend more on medical research and less for weapons.

God bless you, and best of luck.

Sincerely,
N.R.

~~~~~~

Dear Mr. & Mrs. Davids,

Saw the big picture in the So. Bend Tribune of the colored family you had at your farm recently. How foolish can you be? Someday, when they run over your children, just remember you helped.

Whoever told you they have it so rough? They get more from welfare than you and your good Christian neighbors can imagine.

Do you get free food, free clothing, free doctor, free dentist, free rent, free utilities, and your bills paid by welfare?

How many hours a day do you work? I work 12 and don't have what these people do living on welfare. If ever you're in need, try and get welfare - you wouldn't.

I live among these people because of necessity and know just how much they get away with.

Have you ever stopped to think what does he do with his money when he does work? He doesn't work for nothing, or is he a good Christian, too, and does it for nothing?

I'm sure Mr. Sims didn't want to stay in your community because he would have to work to keep up a farm, not put in time like he does at Studebaker's and get help also from welfare.

Please tell me how many of your local unmarried girls with 3 & 4 illegitimate children are living off of welfare, like queens.

Do you have any? If you think I am talking out of turn, just contact the welfare in Newbury, N.Y.

Christianity is fine, but you could have helped a needy white family who can't get welfare.

I am a disgusted tax-payer who thinks you are all wrong. These people wouldn't help each other at all. They wouldn't borrow a penny to each other but get it off the sucker, the white man. Wait till they run you over, then have them come to your farm.

Please give this letter to your children for posterity, and they'll say this woman was right.

It's an old saying, "God helps those who help themselves."

Gee! How lucky you are, we are looking for a community just like yours, who doesn't have any Negroes.

~~~~~~

7-14-61
The Davids
Spring Valley, Minn.

Dear Folks, you certainly made a fine selection when you invited the Sims family.

Any man who was laid off in August and could not find another job must be a mighty lazy man, white or black.

I certainly hope that none of your innocent children will marry one of your visitors. You do not know the Negro.

Sincerely,
R.O.

July 19, 1961

Dear Mrs. Davids:

I wish to congratulate you for your recent act of hospitality in inviting and entertaining the Negro family from my state of Indiana.

I read with interest the news item in our paper and I think it was marvelous of you.

I've always had the greatest respect for the Negro race, and if I had a big home, I'd like to do just what you did.

Yours truly,
G.P.

~~~~~~

July 21, 1961

Mr. & Mrs. Davids,

I read the article in the newspaper and I don't think it was so nice the children loved one another so much.

Just because I am from the South don't think I don't like Negroes. Most people here like the respectable ones.

I do hope your children and the Sims children's love will ripen into matrimony. I think mulattoes are very pretty. I think you would be very happy to have lots of them call you all grandma & grandpa.

A friend

As the following letter was typed and in decent shape, the decision was made to include it as is, minus the name and address, so as to protect the privacy of this brave individual and his family.

~~~~~~

26 July 1961

MARIENUS DAVIES FAMILY
SPRING VALLEY, MINNESOTA
Dear Friends;

I am an American Negro soldier presently stationed here at Fairchild Air Force Base, in the state of Washington. I am writing to you in regard to an article I read in a Seattle Newspaper a few weeks ago while I was attending an Army school there at Fort Lewis.

This article told of your kindness and friendship to a Negro family from New York. That article could only hint at the friendliness and great spirit of true Americanism shown by you, your family and your friends.

I wish to take this opportunity in this er smallest of ways to express my thanks to such a very fine family and wonderful community as yours most certainly is. I am sure that there are many others of my race who would wish to thank you also.

I am a career serviceman and have been on active duty for almost 14 years now and must admit that I have had many doubts as to my purpose in serving my country especially with the racial situation in certain parts of this country. However, I can honestly saythat now I do know why I serve my country, and it is with honor that I do so because of the existance of people like you that I can consider doing so a privilege.

I send my sincerest thanks and appreciation to you, your family and all the people of your community. It is really heartwarming to know of such wonderful people in this great country of ours.

Very truly yours,

July 14, 1961

Dear Mr. and Mrs. Davids,

Thank you so much for the kindness shown to the Sims family. I wish more notice was given to those who are kind to all races. I am a white woman, mother of four. I was visiting my daughter's home in Minneapolis when I saw the article with the pictures in the Minneapolis Star for Saturday evening, July 8.

Whenever I pass a colored person on the street, I try to catch their eye so that I may give them a friendly smile. Perhaps they are afraid of my looking, for about 95% of them avert their faces. But once in a while I can give (and get in return) a kindly smile and word.

Surely, we who truly believe in the Fatherhood of God and the brotherhood of all mankind should be living, shining examples as you folks have been.

I am writing this because, too often, those who are cruel and ruthless write letters to people like you, threatening them or even refusing to employ them if they have been kind.

My prayer is for God to richly bless you for your shining example. This is the hour in which we who believe need to let the Light shine out bright and clear in our daily living.

Sincerely,

L.P.

P.S. My three sons are servicemen and feel as I do about these things before God's sight.

~~~~~~

5 August 1961

Dear Mr. and Mrs. David*,

I am a pre-law student at Michigan State University and a member of their football team. Formerly, I had nothing but sportsmanlike hate for Minnesotans, but you and your Christ-like conduct have made a deep and everlasting impression upon my humble soul.

Like the David of the Old Testament, you are a star that symbolizes leadership. A star that shows singularity and individuality; the same individuality that built this nation.

I prophesize that your example will be the guiding light of others who have been waiting for the Shepherd to show the way, those who have been awaiting the star.

Let me thank you for your daring experiment. You — the Davids — and Miss Mary Miller**, who I'm told has uncolored the Black man with a white heart.

Your community is truly the America that the other states, towns, villages, and communities should emulate.

There are two quotes that I wish to end with, and these are as follows...

"And God said let there be light, and there was light." Genesis 1:3. This is the star of David, you are the light, Mr. and Mrs. David.

"The world is my country, all mankind are my brethren, and to do good is my religion." Thomas Paine, *Rights of Man*.

Finally, in the form of thanks, I wish to confer on you the greatest gift I can bestow. I would give you this name: "Ka'ri wi go", which in Iroquois, which I am, along with being Negro, means "good news." This you undoubtedly are.

Thank you again for your service to humanity and for your indulgence in taking time to read this letter.

I would enjoy hearing from you and hearing of your feelings on the racial problems of our nation.

Dominus Vobiscum

Respectfully,
G.R.

~~~~~~

* The previous author refers to Roselyn and Sharkey as Mr. and Mrs. David. It has not been corrected throughout the letter so as to be in keeping with said author's biblical references to the Star of David and comparisons to this devout duo.

** Mary Miller is the daughter of Don Miller, the "dear friend" referred to in the previous chapter who showed the Sims around Rochester and gave some of them a plane ride. Mary spent much time with the Sims children at the after-church picnic, as well as whenever the Millers visited the farm that week (twice, according to Roselyn's guestbook).

~~~~~~

August 6, 1961

Dear Mr. & Mrs. Davids,

I am so glad that there is a family like yours that I would like to spend a week or two with any time.

I don't know if I'll ever get to spend any time on a farm. But I would love to spend time on yours.

I have a friend that would love to spend a week or a few days on a farm to see how it runs.

D.W.

~~~~~~

August 8, 1961

Dear Mr. and Mrs. Davids,

I am a constant reader of the Jet Magazine and have been for some time, but I was more impressed this week than ever before. The reason I was so impressed was because of the article entitled "Interracial Experiment in Minnesota." In this article, I found it more interesting, as well as enjoyable, to know that after inviting the Sims family to spend a week with you, you said they could live in your house anytime.

I could be wrong – if I am, I hope God will forgive me – but I feel that week was both a help to the Negro and White race.

I noticed in the article that the adjoining neighbors were also friendly to the Sims family and that you said they talked to families that had never talked to Negroes before. I gather from that statement that there aren't any Negro families in or near Spring Valley, Minn. Am I correct?

I must say it looked very good to see your family and the Sims family eating together and also to see your daughter in the picture with the children.

I am a farmer myself and also a Negro, so I guess you can see why I am so proud of that enjoyable week you all were together.

Yours truly,
P.M.

~~~~~~

August 14, 1961

Dear Sir,

We want to thank you for your letter concerning our experiment in Christian Social Relations.

We have had many letters, some positive and some negative. Your letter was unique in that out of all the letters that have registered disapproval, you are the only writer who has had the courage to sign your name. The rest have all been unsigned, many of them insulting.

Even though we do not agree as to how the race problem can be solved, I am glad this is America, where you may believe as you will, and we have the right to entertain in our home these folks that we care to invite.

Thank you again for your letter and for your courage in signing it.

Sincerely,
Mrs. Marienus Davids

~~~~~~

As you can see, the previous letter was sent by Mrs. Davids to the one detractor brave enough to sign his name (the letter dated 7-14-61). Note that she does not lash out at her critic but, instead, thanks him for the letter and expresses gratitude that we live in a country where we can profess differing points of view and invite whomever we like into our homes. To view the content of the repugnant letters not included here would be to truly appreciate her restraint.

The Davids also received many letters from African Americans of a different nature – appeals for help. A few families requested financial aid; others were willing to continue the "Minnesota experiment" in order to spend time on the Davids' farm; some were willing to do what the Sims were not – move lock, stock, and barrel to Spring Valley, providing housing and employment assistance could be furnished. What follows are excerpts from some of these dolorous pleas.

In a letter dated July 10, 1961, I.P. of Indianapolis inked...

"We are a family of fourteen, and I must say that I certainly prefer to live on a farm. I have been trying since I was discharged from the Navy over fifteen years ago to get a farm, but I have never been able to acquire the necessary capital. I am only working part-time, earning less than $30 weekly. I would consider working on a farm for just the necessities (food, shelter, clothing) because I am not earning enough to support the family here. As Christians, we believe the sanctifying grace of God comes from observing his commandments and Christ's teachings. I certainly would like to hear from you and others."

On August 6, 1961, D.C. from Detroit anxiously wrote...

"I have just finished reading about your interracial experiment and, first of all, may I congratulate you and may God bless you. I am a Negro woman with three lovely little girls. I was formerly married to a Methodist minister – we are divorced... I believe my children could be very happy as a part of such a community as yours. I could substitute teach and become an integral participant in your community life. I would appreciate being considered as a possible candidate for the continuance of your interracial experiment. Please mention us to your friends and neighbors... God bless you for your thoughtfulness."

On August 6, 1961, C.B. from Chicago desperately penned...

"... Me and my wife are in very bad condition. We have four children, two of which I am trying to send to school. You see, there are no jobs here, and I cannot find anything to do. We need clothes and shoes and a lot of other important things. We are living in one small room, only one bed. Me and my wife sleep on the floor and let the children sleep on the bed... If there is anything you can do for us, please, I am begging you for help. I got your address from Jet magazine. If you cannot send clothes or shoes, please send a little money for us to buy food... I would much rather come and live in Spring Valley if I can find work and a good church to attend. Please, I am begging you with all my heart and soul, please help me if you can... I am Negro, not that it makes any difference. I am just another family who needs help."

Whether or not Roselyn responded to any of these requests is undetermined, as no such correspondence has been uncovered. Ignoring such supplication would have been difficult, to say the least, given the munificent nature of this remarkable woman.

Chapter 13: The Aftermath

With a U-Haul full of clothes and food in tow, the Sims family headed back to the not-so-green pastures of South Bend. Their trip home would not be uneventful, however. The sharing of memories of scrumptious food, marvelous people, and merrymaking would be interrupted by – you guessed it – car trouble, as Mr. Sims relates in a postcard sent to the Davids.

Note the date – July 15 – and the content. The Sims have already spread the good news to neighbors and friends about their amazing week spent at the Davids' farm, and Mr. Sims elaborates on such in his subsequent letter. He was evidently interviewed by someone at the local South Bend newspaper, as "the Tribune carried the story on the front page of the Sunday edition," according to Sims, though he doesn't mention which Sunday (likely the 23rd). In an earlier Tribune article, Sims is quoted summing up the seven-day stay at the Davids' farm as the "greatest experience of our lives. Something we'll never forget." Sims further pontificates, "It's unbelievable how we were treated. No Negro families live in the Spring Valley area, but all the residents truly greeted us with open arms. It was a great demonstration of what we call friendly, Christian spirit in action."[21]

In his longest letter to date, Sims dishes out a delectable concoction of praise for the Sumner community, mentioning the Millers, Rev. Utzman, and David Pennington by name, mixed with apprehension regarding reporters, calling into question their accuracy in quoting interviewees. While the quotation above may or may not be verbatim, those words perfectly encapsulate his sentiment.

~~~~~~

314 So. Illinois St.
South Bend 19
Indiana July 30, 1961

Dear friends,

As you know, we arrived home safely. Our only difficulty was a burned-out universal joint. This happened in Gary, Indiana, about sixty miles from home. Having limited funds, you know how thankful we were for the funds given to us by the church and the people of your community. Without the funds, it would not have been possible for us to journey home.

---

[21] "Negro Family Praises Visit." South Bend Tribune, July 11, 1961.

On many occasions, Ruby and I have attempted to find words to convey to you folks, your minister, your wonderful friends and neighbors, and all the people we met how our hearts were warmed and refreshed by the fellowship, hospitality, friendship, and love shown our family in your home, church, and by the people in the community. Your people displayed a genuine warmness and friendship that made us feel as welcomed as if we were in our own home church and community.

You have wonderful neighbors and an outstanding young minister; in fact, an outstanding community. You must treasure and guard them with your lives. The spirit that prevailed during our visit has our souls rejoicing as we recall the memories of the various heartwarming experiences. Our short stay in your community gave me the opportunity to explain in our church what effects this visit had on our family. We explained that the visit enriched our lives, uplifted and increased our love, rededicated our devotion, redoubled our strength, and buoyed our determination that, in spite of all the evil that exists in this world, there is still hope that mankind will yet live on this earth in the true image of God as brothers and in peace and happiness.

As we expected, our people were well acquainted with and exceedingly rejoiced by the way your community received us, as the Tribune carried the story on the front page of the Sunday edition. Everywhere we go, our people comment on this. Just goes to prove our belief that there are still some good white people left, referring to the example your community set before the world. Everyone agreed it was the proper thing to do, and they rejoiced at the good news about Negro-White human relations. If the comment puzzles you in any way, you must realize our people's faith and confidence have been unmercifully abused by so many of your people for so long a period of time until even the best of us hesitate to have complete confidence in your people in all fields of endeavor, simply because our confidence has been betrayed on a mass scale and our bitter experiences have taught us that our trust and faith that we gave freely were used to damn future generations to come. In all sincerity, I must say your people in all walks of life, who sincerely believe in the brotherhood of man and the fatherhood of God, must untiringly continue to show by your everyday example that you are sincere in your belief that all men must be free to determine their own destiny in this troubled and tormented world.

Many of our people say, "Our country cannot take one isolated human relations story and convince the world that the leopard has changed its spots," meaning that the good white Christian with enough courage to do what your community displayed is so far and few until the few appear to be losing the battle for democracy to the many. This is why I say efforts must be made by your people on a mass scale to concern themselves about our people's plight throughout the nation, for it will take complete freedom for the Negro in America to convince the African that, should he decide to accept our type of democracy, every man, regardless of color or race, has the equal opportunity to compete in all fields of endeavor.

I am happy to say to you that your people have won the respect and love of all the people of our community by your example. People as far away as Germany are inquiring, "Do you know the Negro family who visited the Whites in Minnesota?" Some of the neighbors who were concerned about our safety commented, "After we read in the paper that everything turned out alright, we were so happy that you went to a heaven and not a hell." Even a six-year-old - when her mother first started to read the story - began to cry, for she feared something had happened to us. But her mother explained that we were having a good time and enjoying ourselves so she was glad. You know how wonderful this made us feel upon our return. I could go on all day quoting comments.

Some of our people felt we were fools to accept the offer your community extended. Even some of my own people don't understand as to why I feel I'm needed here, especially so since I'm not doing so well financially.

Please ask Reverend Utzman to give a special thanks to the people of your community for us. Tell them we are firm believers in the quotation: "The good that you do in the lives of others will someday come into your own." We feel that all of you have truly exalted God's love to its highest peak known to mankind, for what more can you do to prove to mankind that you are sincere. You shared the sacredness of your home, church, and community with us. Even though it was only for a week, our hearts tell us you were pure, devoted, and sincere.

We are honored to have this experience in Christian fellowship, that we hold to be self-evident, that you are truly seeking the road to Christ. These experiences we shall treasure and carry to our graves.

We are enclosing a few clippings to give you a view of our press coverage. I won't bother to go into details as to what I did or did not say, as the reporter supposedly quoted me as saying it would require too much time. His intention was good. But, to my bitter experiences, a lot of the statements he credited me with saying I did not say. God knows I have learned a lesson in dealing with the press. If ever I so much as say "hello" to a reporter again, it will be in writing, with ninety-nine carbon copies. I've heard people talk about misquotes, addition, subtraction, etc. Now I really know what they mean. Please explain to the people who may chance to see the article we have no false pride and certainly did not pretend we did not accept the gifts of money. I called the reporter after he goofed up the story. He explained he was trying in his way to make me look good in the eyesight of the people here. That's why he neglected to say we accepted cash from your people. Personally, it hurt us deeply. We wanted the people to know your people cared enough to share everything they possessed with us, including money, for we felt this wasn't done out of pity but, rather, love for your fellow man who was less fortunate than yourself due to circumstances.

I've received temporary employment with school city. I receive $1.70 per hour. The publicity definitely aided. I will tell more next time.

All send their best in love and fellowship. I wrote Mr. Pennington. As yet, we haven't sent the Millers anything other than a card. You will tell them, as well as the rest, all are in our thoughts and we hope for the best for them all.

Love,
David & Ruby Sims and family

P.S. Thank Mr. Pennington for the personal gifts he and his neighbors contributed for us. We neglected to do so in the letter I mailed to him. Thanks in advance.

~~~~~~

Dear friends,

We are leaving for Iowa in a few minutes. Just want to take a moment to send along the church programs and $10 that belongs to you.

Did you get a copy of Jet magazine for August 10, 1961? It features the pictures taken by Mr. Hale.

My how empty the house seemed when all our little folks were gone. We did enjoy our week's visit with you all so much.

We've received much mail and I hope to share it with you in later letters to you.

We rejoice with you about your new employment.

Thank you for your letter and the clippings. We enjoyed them so much. I shall write at greater length soon. Until then, our love to you all.

Sharkey, Roselyn, Joyce & Gregory

Although the previous letter is not dated, its contents point to it being sent shortly after the reception of Mr. Sims' letter of July 30th.

Around that same time, the Davids received a letter from the Fillmore County Council of Churches, congratulating them on their success in "entertaining the Negro family." This is actually the second of two congratulatory letters sent by the Council. The first was conceived on July 8th. It is basically a lengthier version of this one, plus written in cursive; hence, there was no need to include both.

"Go . . . . . Teach"

FILLMORE COUNTY COUNCIL OF CHURCHES
Working With the
Minnesota Council of Churches

Department of Christian Education
Department of Christian Social Relations

Christian Rural Overseas Program
United Church Women

Office of

Preston _____ . Minn.

Secretary

July 24 1961 , 19___

Dear Mr. and Mrs. Davids and family,

    The Officers of the County Council of Churches wish to thank you and salute you and your family for the magnanimous spirit you have displayed in inviting and entertaining the Negro family so recently with you.

    No doubt this deed done in the interest of better race-relations has enriched your lives and the lives of those about you.

    We commend you and wish God's blessing upon you.

Cordially yours,
Mrs. Donald Aug

A few days earlier, the following letter was sent from Peter Lassally to Mrs. Davids. Though inconclusive, it does seem to answer a question that percolated while researching Bob Considine, one that may also have piqued the reader's curiosity: Did Considine ever write a column for the New York Journal-American outlining the Sims-Davids friendship? It would appear not, a shame given the goodwill it could have fostered.

THE NBC WEEK-END RADIO SERVICE

July 13, 1961

Mr. & Mrs. Marienus Davids
R R #3 Box 100
Spring Valley, Minnesota

Dear Mr. & Mrs. Davids:

I have just returned from a month long vacation and
found your letter on my desk with the good news that
you have finally met with the Sims family.

Since Bob Considine is currently out of the country,
my office could not forward the letter to him. However,
when he does return, I will certainly tell him about
the happy event.

If you have the time, I would certainly love to hear
how everything turned out.

Sincerely,

Peter Lassally
Producer
MONITOR

PL:jp

Notice the letters' header. Some readers may be familiar with the long-running NBC radio show *Monitor*. Running on weekends from 1955-1975, *Monitor* featured a wide array of news, sports, comedy, and even live music remotes. Bob Considine's "On The Line With Considine" was a regular segment. Born of ingenuity and desperation (TV was stealing radio's audience), *Monitor* became wildly successful. Featured guests included such comedy legends as Phyllis Diller, Bob Hope, Woody Allen, and Bob Newhart. Celebrity interviews dotted the broadcast landscape and among them was none other than Roselyn Davids! NBC affiliate KROC out of Rochester (the same station to broadcast *Image: Minorities*) sent Tom Aaker to interview Mrs. Davids. The original script of the questions she was asked by Aaker, faded over time but still legible, is included as a critical piece of Sims-Davids history. As there does not appear to be an archived copy of the program, an attempt will be made to answer the questions in Roselyn's own words, either from information in correspondence with David Sims or from news articles appearing in her scrapbook.

INTERVIEW WITH MRS. MARIENUS DAVIDS OF SUMNER CENTER FOR MONITOR

AUGUST 26, 1961 --- TOM AAKER---KROC---ROCHESTER

WELL--WERE SITTING IN THE SPACIOUS LIVING ROOM AT THE DAVIDS HOME IN SUMNER CENTER MINNESOTA--MRS. DAVIDS, DID YOU HAVE ANY FEARS THAT THE VISIT MIGHT NOT WORK OUT---EVEN THOUGH IT SEEMED LIKE A GOOD IDEA IN THEORY?

DID ANY MEMBERS OF THE SIM'S FAMILY OR YOUR FAMILY FEEL SHY WITH EACH OTHER?

DID YOU HEAR OF ANY OBJECTIONS FROM YOUR NEIGHBORS BEFORE OR DURING THE VISIT?

I UNDERSTAND THE WHOLE COMMUNITY OF SUMNER CENTER BECAME INVOLVED IN THE VISIT. CAN YOU TELL US ABOUT THIS?

WAS THERE ANY FRICTION?

MRS. DAVIDS, I'M SURE MEL AND THE AUDIENCE WOULD LIKE TO KNOW HOW THE CHILDREN OF YOUR TWO FAMILIES GOT ALONG?

DO YOU FEEL---HAVING SPENT A WEEK TOGETHER---THAT THE SIMS ARE YOUR KIND OF PEOPLE?

WOULD YOU SAY THE VISIT WAS A SUCCESS?

WERE ANY OF YOUR IDEAS CHANGED OR DEEPENED OR MODIFIED IN ANY WAY BY THE WEEK YOU SPENT TOGETHER?

The first item of note is the first word of the opening statement: Mel (it should be one L, not two). This refers to Mel Allen, one of many hosts (some of whom went on to become household names, such as Hugh Downs, Art Fleming, and Ed McMahan) to appear on *Monitor* during its 20-year run. Mr. Allen's claim to fame was serving as the play-by-play announcer for the New York Yankees baseball games, both radio and television, from 1940 to 1964, calling 22 World Series during his stint. *Monitor* originally broadcast live non-stop from 8 am Saturday to midnight Sunday, but by 1961, much of the content was prerecorded and the weekend broadcast hours had been slashed to eight each day, with Allen often helming the Saturday morning slot.

Now, on to the questions. The first is easily answered from a story that appeared in the Seattle Post-Intelligencer, in which Roselyn is quoted as saying, "We felt like it was the right thing to do, to invite them, regardless of what the community felt. We knew about these people – they were so wonderful to us when we moved here four years ago. But you can't guarantee a thing like that."[22] The Rochester Post-Bulletin provided a similar quote: "...I thought this would be a way to find out my true feelings on the subject (racism). Would I be able to practice what I had been preaching, and would our community accept a visit from a Negro family?"[23] So any apprehension Roselyn might have felt was not a reflection of how she thought the two families would get along but, rather, how the Sumner community would react.

---

[22] "Minnesotans Show Kindness to Negro Family." Seattle Post-Intelligencer, July 10, 1961.
[23] Pennington, David. Sumner Center White Family, South Bend Negroes Try Human Relations Experiment." Rochester Post-Bulletin, July 7, 1961.

Were family members shy around each other? Given the gravity and circumstances, it is logical to assume that could have been the case early on. But given Roselyn's comments about the children playing together so lovingly practically right away, any initial reticence must have quickly dissipated.

If there were objections raised by neighbors before or during the visit, none were voiced to Mr. and Mrs. Davids directly. Given how the entire Sumner community rallied around the event and showered the Sims with gifts of money, food, and clothes, the notion seems ludicrous.

The fact that this historic event happened at all is a testament to the unity of the Sumner community. Recall that the church folk donated the money necessary to fund the trip in the first place. They sent the Sims home with a trailer full of goods. In between, they invited the Sims children to their homes and various functions, organized and carried out the "picnic in the park" in Spring Valley after the Sunday church service, and conducted a sightseeing tour of Rochester. It was truly a group effort... and a labor of love.

According to the newspaper articles, the only friction that whole week was a brief kerfuffle between the Sims' and Davids' dogs Thursday evening. [24] The snarling ended almost as quickly as it began, thus concluding this fleeting moment of interracial tension (Midnight was a mostly-black stately German Shepherd; the Davids' dog, Tupper, was a pugnacious mixed breed, a "Heinz 57", as a young Gregory

---

[24] Pennington, David. "Sumner Center White Family, South Bend Negroes Try Human Relations Experiment." Rochester Post-Bulletin, July 7, 1961.

170

would later describe her). Interestingly, the details of the swimming pool unpleasantries were revealed courtesy of Charlotte and Carla Diane but never mentioned in any article, even when Mr. and Mrs. Sims were specifically asked about how they were treated during their stay. Perhaps they did not wish to tarnish the overall experience by giving any credence to the actions of a handful of hooligans.

As mentioned above and in more detail earlier in the book, the children happily played together almost instantly. See Chapter 10 for Roselyn's precise quote on the matter. While they didn't mix particularly well with the spiteful swimming pool crowd, the Sims' and Davids' children got along with each other just fine.

Judging from these quotes, it would be safe to say that the Sims are the Davids' kind of people... and vice versa. "After their meeting (in August of '60), "Mrs. Davids said she realized that the Sims 'were our kind of people.'" In the aforementioned Jet Magazine feature, Mrs. Sims reciprocates. "Those are our kind of people. They can live in my house anytime."[25]

Was the visit a success? By any measure, the answer would have to be a resounding 'yes'! In fact, Roselyn characterized the "interracial experiment" in the Gospel Messenger article (Chapter 11) as a "howling success."[26] It is noteworthy that no negative comment made or adverse action taken by anyone personally associated with the

---

[25] "Minn. Whites Praised, Blamed for Having Negro House Guests." Jet Magazine, August 10, 1961.
[26] "Negro Family Guests of Church Couple." Church of the Brethren Gospel Messenger, August 19, 1961, p.23.

events of that impactful week could be found. That speaks volumes.

Mrs. Davids' convictions were formed long before the Sims' visit. Given that the couples had been corresponding for two years and met in August of last year, it is safe to say that the Davids knew exactly what to expect in hosting their South Bend comrades in Christ. The events of that week only reinforced what Roselyn already knew: that there is good in everyone, and it has nothing to do with skin color.

```
 INTERVIEW WITH MRS. DAVIDS CONTINUED)


MRS. DAVIDS, I UNDERSTAND THAT IT WAS A QUOTE FROM A PEARL BUCK
BOOK THAT FIRST SET YOU THINKING ABOUT THIS.  CAN YOU TELL US
WHAT THE QUOTATION WAS?


MRS. DAVIDS, I HAVE REALLY ENJOYED THIS AND I WANT TO THANK YOU
VERY MUCH FOR TALKING WITH US.  WELL, MEL, THAT'S THE STORY FROM
SUMNER CENTER---THIS IS TOM AAKER RETURNING YOU TO MONITOR.


                              -30-
```

The reader has already read the Pearl Buck quote, as it appeared in the *E.U.B. Church News Review* story back in Chapter 11. But it is worth repeating. "How can white men save the souls of the Negro for heaven when they won't let them in their own houses?"[27]

The wording of the Tom Aaker sign-off suggests a live broadcast.

---

[27] "A Freedom Ride with a Different Ending." The Minnesota Conference News Review, August 1961.

However, Roselyn would later convey to Mr. Sims that the interview was recorded on the 26th and would air on September 2nd, to be followed by a similar interview with him, according to a Rochester Post-Bulletin story.[28] Regardless, given the audience of *Monitor*, the most listened-to radio program of that time, both interviews were likely heard by thousands of people!

---

[28] "Sumner Center Farm Couple to Get Urban League Brotherhood Award." Rochester Post-Bulletin, September 1, 1961.

Chapter 14: Sims and Davids' Excellent Adventure

With the Sims-Davids epic encounter in the rear-view mirror, one might conclude that the "climax" of their adventure has come and gone and that the rest of their journey would be just "falling action," to use story element terminology until "resolution" finally occurs. It is true that the goal of Mr. and Mrs. Davids was to host the Sims family with unparalleled hospitality, demonstrating along the way a love that transcended race. Mission accomplished. But so much more needed to be done if this was to become the model for the interaction between Blacks and Whites going forward. The struggles for both families were far from over, but at least, in some small measure, their efforts were about to be recognized and rewarded... and by a nationally renowned organization, no less.

The National Urban League, or NUL, was founded in 1910 in New York City as a vehicle to further the economic, social, and spiritual interests of the Negro population in this country. It steadily expanded in size, scope, influence, and membership to become one of the premiere organizations to fight for the civil rights of Black Americans, though its initial focus was on housing, employment, and education. By 1961, the NUL had dozens of affiliates in several states and was fully engaged in the civil rights movement.[29] As such, the Sims-Davids interracial amity garnered the attention of this prestigious organization, which deemed it necessary to recognize the

---

[29] https://en.wikipedia.org/wiki/National_Urban_League. Wikipedia.

efforts of these two families.

The Urban League's national conference for that year was scheduled to be held in Dayton, Ohio, on Labor Day. Though the schedule of events was already set, NUL president Henry Steeger was resolute about adding one more item to the agenda – an award presented to David and Ruby Sims and Marienus and Roselyn Davids, providing, of course, that they would be willing and able to accept invitations to attend. Said invites were mailed and received but, sadly, are MIA.

~~~~~~

August 22, 1961
314 So. Illinois St.
South Bend 19, Indiana

Mr. Guichard Parris
Conference Secretary
National Urban League
14 East 48th Street
New York, 17, N. Y.

Dear Sir:

Our family received a surprise visit by Mr. and Mrs. Davids on August 18th. During the short stay, we discussed the invitation extended us by your organization to attend the Annual Conference in Dayton on September 4th. Since our family has suffered from prolonged joblessness for such a long period of time, we anticipated traveling to Dayton with the Davids in their automobile. However, they expressed to us while here that they are also hard-pressed for traveling expenses. Mr. Davids, as you know, must pay for care for livestock, etc., during his absence from the farm; not even considering gas, oil, meals, etc., while traveling to the city.

Inasmuch as we rejoice and count it a great honor to be considered worthy of the citation, unless both families could be provided with traveling expenses, which would amount to about $25.00, we feel we can't afford to attend.

With highest regard, love, and dedicated devotion to your stated principal: equal opportunity.

Sincerely,
Mr. and Mrs. David Sims

It would seem Sharkey and Roselyn not only received their invitation but felt the need to discuss with David and Ruby in person the logistics of what a weekend trip to Dayton would look like should they accept. This short visit was documented in a previously cited Rochester Post-Bulletin article. "The Davids visited them at their home... and were welcomed by about sixty of the Sims' friends at a dinner in the all-Negro neighborhood."[30] Not much else is known about the short stay, but both couples agreed on two things: they were deeply honored to be recognized in such a fashion by one of the premiere organizations to fight for what they believed in, and that travel expenses and the costs of hiring a dependable farmhand while

---

[30] David Pennington, "Sumner Center White Family, South Bend Negroes Try Human Relations Experiment," Rochester Post-Bulletin, July 7, 1957.

the Davids were away would make such a trip unfeasible.

After the merriment subsided, the compassionate couple returned to their halcyon homestead, resigned to the premise that a date with Dayton was probably not in the cards. Imagine Roselyn's surprise when she received a notification from the Urban League that would make the trip possible after all! She immediately put pen to paper to notify Mr. Sims of the good news.

~~~~~~

August 26, 1961
R.R. #3 Box 100
Spring Valley, Minn.

Dear friends,

We received a call from the Urban League last night saying they would take care of the financial end of our trip, so we are planning to make the trip.

If it is OK with you, we could plan to be at your place about 1:00-1:30 on Sunday afternoon, September 3rd.

KROC, the NBC station in Rochester, sent one of their newsmen out Saturday and recorded an interview that will be heard on Monitor next Saturday. I suppose the South Bend station came to your place.

Hope you are all well. Thank you so much for the children's birthday cards. We are looking forward to seeing you soon.

Love from all of us,
Sharkey, Roselyn, Joyce, and Gregory

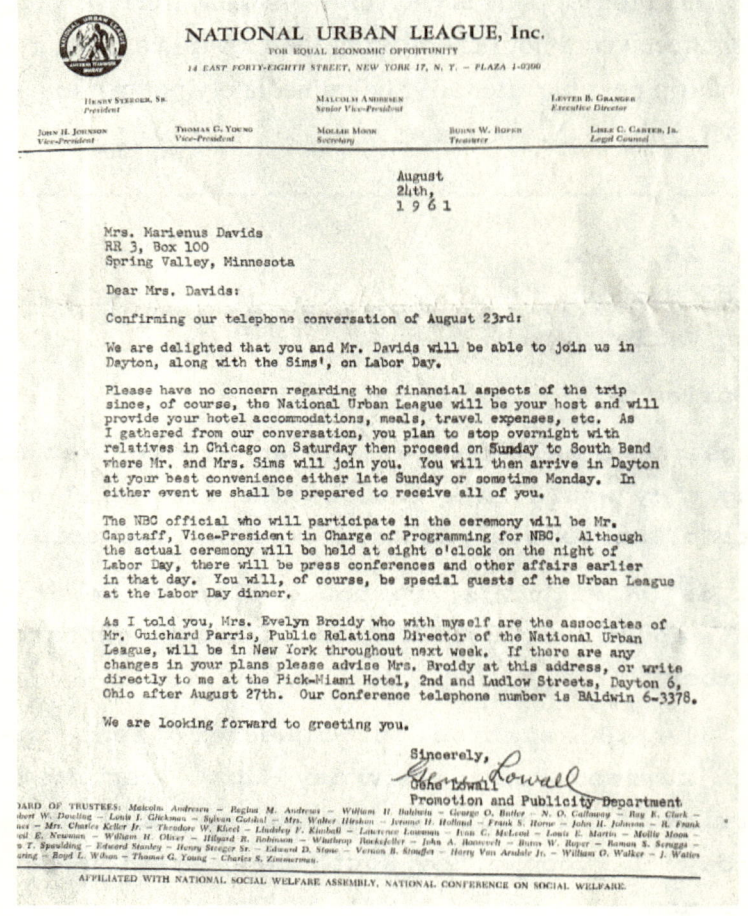

August
24th,
1961

Mrs. Marienus Davids
RR 3, Box 100
Spring Valley, Minnesota

Dear Mrs. Davids:

Confirming our telephone conversation of August 23rd:

We are delighted that you and Mr. Davids will be able to join us in Dayton, along with the Sims', on Labor Day.

Please have no concern regarding the financial aspects of the trip since, of course, the National Urban League will be your host and will provide your hotel accommodations, meals, travel expenses, etc. As I gathered from our conversation, you plan to stop overnight with relatives in Chicago on Saturday then proceed to South Bend where Mr. and Mrs. Sims will join you. You will then arrive in Dayton at your best convenience either late Sunday or sometime Monday. In either event we shall be prepared to receive all of you.

The NBC official who will participate in the ceremony will be Mr. Capstaff, Vice-President in Charge of Programming for NBC. Although the actual ceremony will be held at eight o'clock on the night of Labor Day, there will be press conferences and other affairs earlier in that day. You will, of course, be special guests of the Urban League at the Labor Day dinner.

As I told you, Mrs. Evelyn Broidy who with myself are the associates of Mr. Guichard Parris, Public Relations Director of the National Urban League, will be in New York throughout next week. If there are any changes in your plans please advise Mrs. Broidy at this address, or write directly to me at the Pick-Miami Hotel, 2nd and Ludlow Streets, Dayton 6, Ohio after August 27th. Our Conference telephone number is BAldwin 6-3378.

We are looking forward to greeting you.

Sincerely,

John Lowall

Promotion and Publicity Department

Shortly thereafter, the Davids would receive this confirmation from the NUL, verifying the organization's desire to pay any and all expenses related to the trip, as well as details of the convention itinerary.

According to this letter, the Davids likely embarked on their Ohio odyssey on Saturday, September 2nd. After an overnight with the Millers in Villa Park, the tireless twosome would motor on to South Bend the next day, arriving early afternoon. Details are sketchy after that, as none of the Sims siblings remember much about this visit and did not accompany the adults to the convention. As the NUL conference was Monday, September 4th, and Dayton was but a four-hour drive, departing early Labor Day morning would have likely been the choice were it not for the NUL's generous offer to pick up the tab; consequently, a Sunday night stay at the Pick-Miami Hotel (one of 17 Albert Pick hotels, famous for their hospitality) may have been too tempting to pass up, especially with the elegant establishment hosting the big event.

The next day bustled with speeches and presentations as around 500 conference attendees were entertained and enthralled by the colloquium's activities. Amongst them, of course, was the bestowing of NUL's "Friendship and Neighborliness" (or "Brotherhood and Citizenship", depending on the news source) Award to each couple. That the presentation was made by none other than the aforementioned NUL president, Mr. Steeger, only added to the prestige of receiving such recognition. NBC was honored in a similar fashion for its role in augmenting the long-distance interracial friendship, with Mr. A. L. Capstaff, vice-president for radio programs, accepting the citation on behalf of the network.[31] The

---

[31] "Friendship and Neighborliness," Urban League Newsletter, Autumn 1961.

symposium's main address was delivered that evening by Mr. Lester Granger, who would soon thereafter retire from the NUL after serving as its executive director for twenty years.[32]

In a Q&A shortly after the convocation's conclusion, a gracious Mrs. Davids remarked, "We feel very humble being chosen to receive this award. Some people have sacrificed much more, even shed blood, to improve race relations. All we did was have fun while the Sims and their children were visiting us."[33]

When asked to sum up the affair, she would later respond, "It's so much more than just the award. It's been a rich, overwhelming experience."[34]

---

[32] "Spring Valley Area Couple Gets Award," Rochester Post-Bulletin, September 5, 1961.
[33] "Sumner Center Farm Couple to Get Urban League Brotherhood Award," Rochester Post-Bulletin, September 1, 1961.
[34] "League Award Given White, Negro Families," Dayton Journal Herald, September 5, 1961.

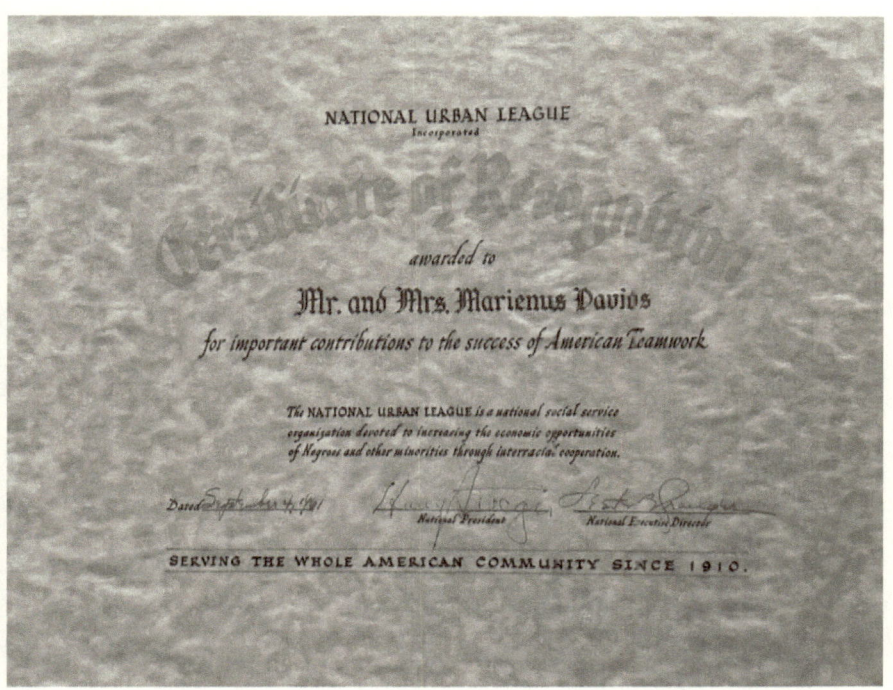

A fair amount of sightseeing was also undertaken by the Sims and Davids while they were in Dayton, though it is not clear as to when that took place. Given how busy both couples must have been on Monday with the conference activities, it is fair to assume that the quartet spent Tuesday exploring the city. This included, according to one source,[35] an interview on NBC's "Today" TV show, although this cannot be confirmed. Regardless, the local NBC affiliate supposedly broadcast a recorded version of the awards presentation from the previous day. Then, it was off to Central State College, which, at the time, was lauded as a model of integration. This was the main site

---

[35] "Sumner Center Farm Couple to Get Urban League Brotherhood Award," Rochester Post-Bulletin, September 1, 1961

both couples were interested in visiting while in Dayton, and for good reason.

Now known as Central State University (as of 1965), this iconic institution of higher learning began in 1887 as merely a department within Wilberforce University (founded in 1855 and the first university to be owned and operated by African Americans, via the African Methodist Episcopal Church) as a two-year course for industrial education. In 1947, it blossomed into a four-year program with an emphasis on teacher training, hence Roselyn's interest (she graduated from Iowa State Teachers College – now the University of Northern Iowa – in 1951). Known then as the Combined Normal and Industrial Department, it broke from Wilberforce and established its own campus, changing its name to Central State College in 1951.[36]

The fervent foursome apparently visited many other sites – historical and otherwise – throughout the city, as well as meeting with various government officials, Central State U officers, and, of course, NUL VIPs. No details, however, are documented other than what appears in the photo captions.[37]

---

[36] Central State University. (2024, September 24). In Wikipedia. https://en.wikipedia.org/wiki/Central_State_University
[37] "Spring Valley Area Couple Gets Award," *Rochester Post-Bulletin*, September 5, 1961.

BUSY DAY IN DAYTON—During their Labor Day visit as NUL
Annual Conference guests, the Sims' and Davids' were taken
on tour of places they wished to visit together. Left: Greeted

on Central State College campus by President Charles H.
Wesley. At right: Relaxing in hotel suite after sightseeing and
visiting points of interest in Dayton area.

183

Although the exact timeline is not known, one source[38] claims that the Davids headed home on Wednesday but does not mention from where. As traversing the entire 680-mile route back to their farm from Dayton by way of South Bend would be a minimum of twelve hours, but probably longer, given the inevitable stops for meals, gas, and, of course, dropping the Sims off at their home, a one-day trip seems unlikely. Perhaps the eclectic excursionists, after a pit stop in South Bend to drop off their traveling compadres, ventured on to Villa Park so that, after a restful overnight at the Millers, they would have a more manageable drive the next day. As the particular circumstances of the journey home seem to be lost to the annals of time, much like the sightseeing specifics, they will most likely remain – in the immortal words of William Shatner (said with a slight whisper) – unexplained.

---

[38] "Spring Valley Area Couple Gets Award," Rochester Post-Bulletin, September 5, 1961.

Chapter 15: Speak of The Devil

The renown that resulted from the newspaper coverage of the July and September events took many forms. In addition to the hate mail and pleas for aid, requests to speak at various functions were becoming commonplace for these two vanguards and would continue for years to come. For Mr. Sims, this often meant a foray into hostile territory, either to do battle with city or state officials on behalf of his brethren or to attempt to persuade others of his kind that not all Whites are devils (which he elaborates on in his upcoming letter). Mrs. Davids' invocations, on the other hand, came mainly from local churches, as congregations were hungry for knowledge of her experience and inspiration on how best to apply her God-given spirit of beneficence to their local community, as well as improve attitudes about race relations. Three such examples follow.

~~~~~~

October 18, 1961

Dear Mrs. Davids,

Our meeting will be held on November 7th at 8 pm at xxxx (name and address omitted for privacy reasons). We will be looking forward to seeing you and hearing your wonderful story.

Sincerely,
Pat Pennington

If that last name looks familiar, it should. Pat is the wife of David Pennington, the author of many of the Rochester Post-Bulletin articles cited in this book. The talented twosome was crucial to the telling of this incredible story in multiple ways: David wrote the newspaper articles, reciting details of those eventful days in Dayton and Sumner Center, many of which would otherwise be lost or forgotten. Pat organized the October 18th meeting that Roselyn spoke at (as well as many other unrelated charitable events), and together, they contributed a number of items that ended up in South Bend via the U-Haul rental, something Mr. Sims gratefully acknowledged in a previous letter.

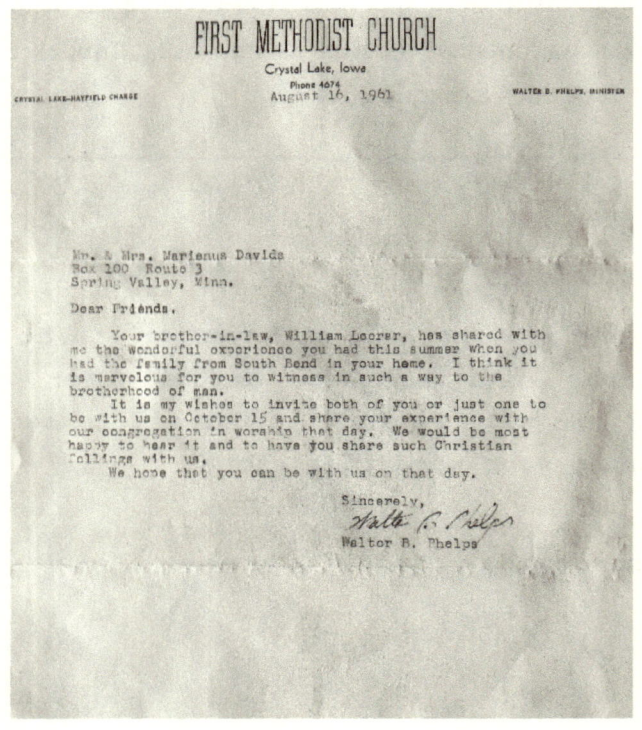

Preston, Minnesota
July 29, 1962

Dear Mrs. Davids,

I am writing in regard to getting you to speak at our women's fellowship meeting of the Church of the Brethren on September 13th at 2 pm. I have heard much about you and your activities from the paper and from members of our group who have heard you speak. We want a guest speaker for the final meeting of our present church year to inspire us to do more for others as our new church year is about to begin. You were highly recommended for such a task.

If that date doesn't fit your schedule, we could adjust our meeting date to fit your schedule.

Our church is located in rural Preston. I will send exact directions if you can come.

I hope you will be able to come. The reports... which have been passed on to us have made me most anxious to meet you and to hear you.

Sincerely,
Mrs. C.B.

Note the date on the letter. While out of order chronologically, it is in keeping with the subject matter and is included to demonstrate the scope of Mrs. Davids' influence and the excitement generated in those anxious to hear her speak.

The next piece of correspondence between Mr. Sims and Mrs. Davids is dated November of '61. The only other letter during this period of time is a thank-you from the Davids addressed to Mr. Steeger of the NUL, which appears below. While every other hand-written letter has been transcribed to "Courier New" font to make it legible yet still convey the feeling of having been hammered out on a vintage Underwood typewriter, it would be a crime to allow Roselyn's exquisite handwriting to suffer such a fate. Given that the letter was well-preserved, the magnitude of her gratitude is best expressed in its original form.

314 So. Illinois St.
South Bend 19, Indiana
November 5, 1961

Marienus, Roselyn, & family,

Dearest friends, we were happy to hear that you had a safe journey home. We felt that something had you preoccupied. It was a relief to hear that everyone was alright. Of course, our hearts grieved to hear of little Joyce's illness. It may console her to know that our entire church sent up a silent prayer after I told our minister about her illness, as you described it in the letter.

Each Sunday, our church always prays for the sick, less fortunate, etc., so she was included special this morning. We sincerely hope God will be merciful and spare her any health impairment.

We are thankful that her studies and her nursing care are in God's hands, as you pointed out in the letter. These are God's blessings you can count.

One of my classmates stated that she was a member of a cooperative insurance group that she has been set up for from families. She stated the rate was very reasonable. If you aren't already covered, it may pay you to investigate this plan. She also stated that this insurance is rather new and isn't generally known. This information came out in a class discussion of foreign governments and co-ops.

We received a letter from Mrs. Bussman. We haven't answered because the letter was misplaced. We are enclosing a few lines for them. We hope you don't mind as we no longer have their address.

Here in South Bend, the Tribune carried our reception of the given award in a news item special to the Tribune. As one of the contributors to the Voice of the People column, I was given an invitation to the paper's annual dinner, where readers have the opportunity to quiz local and state government officials. It was quite interesting.

We are so happy to hear that others are interested in sharing our experiences through your speaking engagements. Knowing you, we are confident you are doing a good job of promoting better race relations.

The publicity of our visit has created new friends for us. Everywhere we go, people say, "This must have been a wonderful experience for you. If these people ever come here again, we would like to meet them." Or "Why didn't you let us know they were here? We would have enjoyed preparing a dish for them." Our people are very anxious to play host to you folks in response to the wonderful reception your community gave our family. They will not be content until the hospitality is returned by this community. In their words, "We must show Spring Valley we, too, have Christian love to share, and we desire to share our fellowship with them."

Taking stock, Ruby and I are convinced that a new effort – a new approach – has been taken to race relations by the very conservative Saint Joseph

Council of Churches in our area as a direct result of the publicity of the visit.

I was extended an invitation to attend a Muslim Temple meeting after we returned from Dayton. This wasn't my first time there, so I knew pretty much what to expect. I accepted, and while there, I was given a chance to speak about my visit with "you devils" in the language of the speaker who introduced me (smile). Of course, I committed the cardinal sin when I said we were treated royally by everyone we met and that we knew from personal experience that there are some good white people. "If Allah (the living God) says you can't live in peace with the white devils, who are you to question it? You are telling us there are some good white people? Damn you and your good white people, too. If you don't like what I say, I got some brothers here who will back me up if you want to do battle."

Since I was the only Christian among a crowd of approximately forty Muslims, who they had pretty hepped up, I decided the easiest way out was the best; in fact, the only way out, so I refused to say, "Brothers, you are very undemocratic here. You give me the chance to speak my opinion and now you are violently angry with me because I spoke in a manner in which you did not approve." Realizing they would not permit me to say this, I simply smiled, took my seat, and acted gentlemanly.

"How come these devils just now want to get together with you? They had four hundred years to get together with you, didn't they? And why did the devil have to come five hundred miles to invite you into his home? We have a thousand of them right here in South Bend, Indiana, don't we?"

By this time, I was sickened by the idea that my people have to submit to a closed society of this nature because here, they are told they are needed – they are wanted – somebody cares. They must join the Brotherhood and do something for themselves.

Make no mistake about it, the Muslims are doing a wonderful job of teaching our people thrift and unity, how to pool their meager resources for the good of the nation, or brotherhood. They have their own schools, farms, businesses, etc., which is good as far as economic independence is concerned. But the fantastic things they tell our people who haven't had the opportunity to receive a decent education scares me. It is very true - the only thing they tell our people are the brutal crimes that have been committed by your people against us while claiming to be a "Christian, God-fearing nation." This is their theme: "You've been a Christian all of your life. What do you own? Where can you go? Is it not the Christian white man who lynched you? Who raped your women? Who placed you in slavery? Come into Islam, where there is peace, equality, and justice. Come unto your own. The white man wants no part of you, only to further enslave you. Separation, not integration, is the answer."

Another thing they have in their favor is the crimes some of our incompetent, untrained, unchristian, so-called ministers conduct in private and public: alcoholic beverages, misappropriation of funds, etc. Of course, these may be small, isolated incidents, but it gets national attention in the Muslim world.

There is only one reason why our people — what few there are — join a movement of this nature, and that is why they are being shown that they, too, can enjoy a measure of collective, unified action and pooling of their resources. In view of the fact that the majority of those unemployed are our people and the aged, and because local and state officials have no desire to pay for relief for unemployed people, our people are being forced to seek a way out of this crisis. And I fearfully tell you: unless the Christian Whites and the Christian Negroes concern themselves about the plight of our people, when we get around to it, it may be too late. Our people are fast losing confidence in Christian ministers because of their silence, while we have no jobs, go hungry, etc. in a land of plenty.

Please don't be alarmed by what I have written. This condition can be eliminated by Whites and Negroes concerned enough to do their very best to make democracy work for all Americans, for in the best analysis, this is all our people are seeking.

193

I'm confident that there are hundreds of thousands
of communities such as yours who are willing and
wanting to make our religion, our government, and
our nation a living reality: truly, a government
for the people, by the people, and of all the
people, that shall not perish from this Earth.

Love,
The Sims family (answer soon)

~~~~~~

It is astonishing how upbeat Mr. Sims remained despite all the hardships endured by his family and friends. Much of the positivity no doubt stems from the way he and his family were treated by the "white devils" of Sumner Center. No amount of browbeating by cynics would crush his enthusiasm or dampen his love for fellow Christian brothers and sisters, regardless of color or creed. Sims addresses this and other topics in his latest epistle with his usual fervor, but one is left to wonder about the extent of Joyce's illness. Since this is the first time it has been mentioned by either party, it is safe to assume that the letter from Mrs. Davids that Mr. Sims references is MIA. Remember, she would write two identical letters, one she would send to the Sims, the other (not always dated) she would keep in her collection, along with the letters she received from Mr. Sims. This assemblage of correspondence is seemingly not complete, hence the need to further elaborate on the subject.

Joyce was out playing in the yard one September evening, nothing out of the ordinary. Her mom called her into the house for supper. When Joyce didn't come in – unusual for her – Mrs. Davids went out to investigate. There sat little Joyce in the grass. "I can't get up. My legs wouldn't work," she uttered, dismayed and confused. Roselyn instinctively knew something was wrong and called for her husband, who was Johnny-on-the-spot in mere moments. Sharkey carried her into the house while Roselyn called the family physician. Doctor Risser, who was a member of the Sumner Center Church, was at home but agreed to immediately meet the Davids at his office. The initial exam proved inconclusive, but the good doctor had his suspicions, which were later confirmed by further testing – Joyce had rheumatic fever. At that time, the cause and cure were unknown, and this dreaded disease was often fatal. Joyce would be bedridden for months, having thus far completed but three weeks of her kindergarten school year. She endured excruciating pain from both the illness and the weekly injections. Any accidental bumping of the bed she lay in caused her to cry out and writhe in agony. She asked her heavenly father to take her home, and doctors agreed that this would likely be the outcome. Despite the bleak prognosis, her parents refused to give up. Anyone whom they knew was solicited to pray on Joyce's behalf. In James 5:16, the Bible says, "The prayer of a righteous man availeth much." And righteousness was one quality these two had in spades. Anyone who knew Roselyn felt as if she had a direct line to the Almighty because when she prayed, things happened. When asked to accept the inevitable, she would shake her head and respond, "My God is bigger than that." As time passed, Joyce began to show slight improvement. The suffering subsided ever so slowly, finally to the point where she could stand, first with help but eventually by herself. Doctors called it a miracle, the "worst case they'd ever seen of rheumatic fever that wasn't fatal." Everyone was surprised by Joyce's miraculous recovery... everyone, that is, except for Sharkey and Roselyn. They didn't pray, hoping for a miracle; they expected one... and their faith was rewarded. They simply would not accept that five years is all they would get here on Earth with their precious daughter. This simply could not be God's plan for Joyce... and it wasn't. With a case this extreme, Joyce was expected to have severe scarring on her heart... yet she had none. Amazingly, Joyce returned to school in late January of 1962. She took it easy at first, as the Davids were told to limit her physical activity – anything that would stress her heart was off limits. But, in a couple of months, she was playing at recess like any other child. Joyce did her fair share of farm chores as she grew older and, in middle and high school, participated in choir, band, and cheerleading. For those who would claim God is dead or doesn't exist or that healing miracles only happened in Biblical times, this author would beg to differ.

The Sims children were also very concerned about Joyce, so much so that Charlotte took it upon herself to write specifically to Joyce and Gregory (rather than Aunt Roselyn and Uncle Sharkey, as they were affectionately called).

~~~~~~

314 So. Illinois St.
South Bend 19, Indiana

Dear Joyce and Gregory,

How are you both doing? Fine, I hope. Everyone was sorry to hear about you being sick, Joyce. We are glad to hear that you are doing better. The little bit of time you had in kindergarten – how did you like it? Do you remember your teacher's name? If so, what is it?

196

Gregory – I bet you are having fun helping Daddy with the chores. How is Debbie the cow doing? We sure do miss you both, especially Avard. All he talks about is Joyce and Gregory in Minnesota. He told me to say a special "hi" from him. Cheryl and Freda will be writing you soon.

Yours truly,
Charlotte, Avard, Belinda, & family

P.S. (to Aunt Roselyn & Uncle Sharkey) I guess maybe Santa Claus will have to give Greg his rifle.

~~~~~~

As is often the case with such correspondence, many unanswered questions remain. When was this letter written? While there is no date (and no envelope with a postmark), the reference to Santa giving Greg his rifle would indicate sometime prior to Christmas 1961. Charlotte makes mention of being glad that Joyce is doing better, which was the case by then, but the road to returning to normalcy would still be littered with potholes. Where did she get that notion? Another lost Roselyn letter? If so, perhaps a mindful mother passed on a glimmer of hope to her "nieces and nephews" in South Bend. Did Cheryl and Freda write to the Davids? Quite possibly, although no evidence of such can be found. Given that several letters reference matters not found in this collection of communiqués, perhaps those letters, like so many others written by Roselyn and the Sims children, are stashed away in some shoebox, along with other relics, sitting on a shelf in someone's basement or attic, collecting dust, just waiting to be discovered.

Chapter 16: New Year, Same Problems

Jan. 4th, 1962
314 So. Ill. St.
So. Bend 19, Ind.

Dear Marienus, Roselyn, & family,

The delay in responding to your last letter was necessary because: 1) Our minister has been extremely busy with holiday sermons, insurance, etc.; and 2) Mr. Brown, our league's director, is in the process of preparing the 37th annual year's end report, which will be held on January 12th. In as much as it was a necessity for me to discuss the items you listed with them, obviously, you understand our predicament. At this time, I'm happy to report your suggestion has met with favor and joy. Our minister and Mr. Brown approve of and consider your suggestions as concrete and practical ideas.

As yet, I have not been able to visit with Dr. Chamblee. However, he told me several months ago he would be happy to exchange correspondence with your Dr. Risser, so I am enclosing one of his cards. If you would be so kind as to see that the doctor gets the mailing address, we would be very appreciative. At a later date, we will forward to you a complete plan on a community-wide basis. My minister and Mr. Brown wish to broaden the scope and get as much community participation as possible. In order to do this, it will take a little time. Oh, if you think your doctor doesn't consider it improper, you may suggest that I said my doctor has expressed his willingness to exchange greetings and become acquainted with him so I'm sure he would be happy to hear from him. Now, about Rev. Utzman and my minister meeting to lay out a plan: this will all be considered at the meeting, which will take place next week. Mr. Brown suggested we outline a few ideas and he would be glad to participate.

All of us wish and pray for the best for the new arrival. Ruby plans to write you more about the matter later. We've all been wondering if it had arrived yet. Charlotte was thrilled to receive the painting set. She completed an assignment for school with it. She also plans to write you folks. Please explain to all the wonderful people who forward us cards and gifts that we definitely appreciate their thoughtfulness. Our only regret is that since we received so many, it will take quite some time for us to answer them. In the meantime, we know you will pinch-hit for us. Without going into details, just tell Spring Valley that their acts of kindness and thoughtfulness rejoice in our hearts beyond the expression of words. Also tell the Millers and your minister that they will be hearing from us shortly. You may tell the Utzmans that all of our friends and neighbors are presently searching South Bend for the game called "Blockhead." We have enjoyed it so much, as do our friends. In fact, we can't keep it at home. When our friends' friends visit them, they want to use the game for entertainment.

Recently, I returned to work. But as you probably know, we are on strike, not by choice but by company action. S.P. has no desire or need to keep us on the payroll. They have enough cars on reserve to supply dealers for two and a half months. Our union heads were aware of this company stockpiling for months. However, they chose to do nothing about it. We are forced to suffer as a result of their inaction. Unions today do not have the interest of the membership at heart. The company pays our leaders their salaries. They sacrifice our rights for their own personal wealth. This hits us at a bad time, too. Already, we are six hundred dollars in the rear with our house notes. My creditors have threatened to foreclose. Fourteen months of unemployment leaves one in this type of predicament. We pray for the best.

We received a letter from the Don Miller family – we owe them a reply. As soon as possible, I will answer his letter. Tell Marienus he doesn't realize what peace and contentment he enjoys being an independent farmer, secure from the frightful month of no income and the constant need to spend money that you can't secure. City life, or urban living, is not for the poor.

Will you forward a copy of the print that you
stated the E.U.B. was going to use? As of yet, we
haven't had the chance to see one. I am trying to
get a copy of our stay in Dayton to forward to you
folks. As soon as we get one, we will forward it to
you.

Please say hello to your immediate neighbors – the
Kings, the Snyders, the Bussmans – and all the rest
of the wonderful people in your community. How are
Joyce and Greg? We certainly hope they are OK. We
wish for you and yours God's many blessings in the
New Year. Hope to hear from you soon.

With all our love, friendship, and devotion.

Sincerely,
David & Ruby Sims and family

Much to comment on here. What items and suggestions from Mrs.
Davids that Mr. Sims references in the first paragraph are a mystery
but most likely involve his church's methods going forward to
improve the lives, both financially and spiritually, of its congregation,
which one gets the impression is all, or at least mostly, Black.

The "new arrival" mentioned in paragraph three is Patricia Roselyn
Davids, born January 28, 1962. So, as of the writing of this letter, it
would be a little over three weeks before this newest sibling of Joyce
and Gregory would officially make her mark as the third child of
Marienus and Roselyn. As an interesting side note, the caring couple
had been advised not to have more children, as complications with the
first two births resulted in C-sections. But, just as with Joyce's

201

illness, fervent prayer was answered and Patricia was born happy and healthy, though she also came into this world via the same procedure. The doctors insisted Roselyn have no more natural childbirths, as the next one could prove fatal. While she did heed this warning, both parents felt their family was not yet complete and would eventually travel to Korea to adopt a brother (Jonathan) and a sister (Maureen) for Joyce, Greg, and Patricia. The story behind how this came about is, in itself, the subject of another book and is yet another illustration of the love and compassion shown by this marvel of motherhood and her heavenly husband.

The most alarming news shared by Mr. Sims is the potential foreclosure of his family's house. While the Davids were undoubtedly aware of the Sims' grim financial situation, they may not have realized it was this dire. Before Roselyn could respond, Mr. Sims put pen to paper once more.

~~~~~~

Jan. 11, 1962
314 So. Ill. St.
So. Bend, Ind.

Mr. and Mrs. Davids,

Dearest friends – the threatened legal action referred to in our last letter to you folks will occur on Monday, Jan. 15, 1962. Legal proceedings to evict our family will take place. This is what it means to be without a job for 14 months and be dependent upon a relief agency. I returned to work the last week in October. Eight and one-half weeks of unemployment is all I have been able to secure since Aug. 30, 1960, with the exception of six weeks for school city after returning from our visit to your community. At this time, our only salvation lies with God and in the hearts of our people.

As you know, we are on strike at S.P. Corporation. It appears as though it will last until spring. The corporation stated in the Tribune that, presently, they have 20,000 cars in dealers' inventories, enough to supply them for 70 days. At this time, they have no desire to bargain in good faith. We are in a very bad situation. Our union officials tolerated this condition. They were well aware of the fact that the company was stockpiling cars in preparation for a long strike. This is why we rank-and-file know our leadership does not have our best interests at heart. It grieves my heart to realize how cruel and corrupt people can become for money and material gains. The principles that unions were founded upon are being totally disregarded for the almighty dollar by selfish men. We are forced to do picket duty in sub-zero temperatures simply because they did not stop excessive overtime work since the new model was introduced. We can get $25 per week in strike benefits from the International. You can see the predicament that we are in.

If we were not on strike, our situation here would be the same as far as being evicted is concerned. The corporation holding our contract has every legal right to repossess, inasmuch as we are several months in default with the payment schedule. This

203

was accomplished by the illegal policy of the overseer of the poor in direct violation of the state law, which clearly states that indigents (the unemployed) are to be provided adequate basic necessities: food, clothing, shelter, medical attention, etc. so as to maintain recipients in a healthy state. However, they flout the law by setting up inadequate budgets (as in our case). My unemployment insurance for the last six months was income that could only be supplemented and set up on this budget: $144 unemployment insurance per month; $112 food budget; total monthly budget: $256. After a bitter experience, we pointed out that it was impossible for us to maintain health and pay rent, utilities, insurance, etc. on this amount. We showed the agency that if our diet consisted of meatballs and spaghetti, neck bone soup, and cereal on milk twice a day, three meals a day at current costs would be $7.26, or $50.82 per week, or $203.28 per month. This allows nothing for citrus fruits, leafy vegetables, salt, etc. This leaves $52.72 to pay $60 per month rent, plus utilities, insurance, etc. Obviously, it is needless for me to say why we could not pay our house note. Feeding our children was our primary job. This is why we charge the agency with our present plight. They were aware of our situation, but in the interest of the rate down, they sacrificed countless lives. This is the inhumanity of relief administration in our state.

Apathy is widespread among the taxpaying citizens. The only ones concerned about the condition, really, are those of us who, because of unemployment, must rely on it for our existence. This is why I mention that the greatest threat facing our people is slow starvation due to loss of income.

Today, reaction is being applied against us because of our unyielding fight against the corrupt city and county official policy of abusing and refusing our people the bare necessities of life. I have often wondered why the intelligent or educated among us remain silent while our people are being destroyed. It is clear to me now. The forces that control corruption are in high places in local government. Believe me when I say that these people will not hesitate to kill us or destroy anyone who persists in challenging the system. So, we choose to remain silent and stay alive rather than to be vocal and dead.

Here are some of my recent experiences being a pauper. I was forced to go to legal aid (attorney for the poor) with my eviction notice. Having previous bad experiences with this office, I knew I could not expect aid, but faced with no money, I had no other choice. The attorney whom I was seeking legal aid from flatly stated to me, "Sims, if you used your talents properly, you wouldn't be in this predicament," meaning, faced with eviction, "You could earn a lot more than $100 a week at

Studebakers. You know how to play the game. You know what's going on," referencing Uncle Tom Negroes who get political jobs downtown and aid in furthering the degradation of their own people for their own economic security. I stated to this man that I had no desire to do anything illegal or disgraceful. This man is just one of many who have approached me – in so many words – to join the clique. They have not been successful in buying me or completely destroying me with economic pressure.

Their last stage is violence. Many of my people are warning me, "You are treading a dangerous path." The very one I am trying to help will not aid me in a showdown right now. In referring to my plight: "You face eviction. How many have offered you a dollar?" One person told me that the talk going around is that only Communist whites associate with Negroes and accept them as equals. They simply cannot comprehend a friendship of mutual respect and Christian love that we hold for each other and humanity in general.

Years ago, I was laid off, time after time, losing every job I was able to secure. Even then, I was fighting injustice. The aforementioned person also told me that pressure is being applied about my home. He stated that once I return to work, I may even be fined at my place of employment. So, inasmuch as several of my people have told me to be careful and watch out, I must be in line for something. However, my faith is in God;

righteousness will prevail. Will our people come to our rescue? Now that the brunt of reaction has set in, reliable people have stated that people downtown were awake at nights, figuring ways and means to stop Sims, referring to my letters of protest, fighting in Commissions Courts, appealing to the medical association, civic groups, etc. They are determined to stop this crusade. If one thousand of my people would invest $5.75 of their money, they could buy this property and permit us to reimburse them. The question is: can I get the needed support? Our immediate need is $650 by Monday to stop possession by default. With two days to appeal for aid, will one hundred of them loan this family $6.50 a piece, with only a promise that I will pay it back some day after the strike is over and I am able to return to work? These are the questions that only God and the hearts of humanity can answer. Our hopes and fate rest in God's hands. We pray He will deliver us. Give our best wishes of God's blessing to all our friends.

We remain, as always - love and devotion,

David & Ruby Sims family

An uneasy Ruby, obviously concerned for the welfare of her husband, wrote Roselyn regarding the heavy burden he carried.

Jan. 14, 1962
314 So. Ill. St.
So. Bend, Ind.

Dear friends,

First of all, I would like to thank you for the
nice paint set. Roselyn, I bet your box was filled
with Christmas greetings with wrong addresses from
me. I'm sorry. I got some of the addresses mixed
up. Charlotte sent a special thank-you for the set.
I was so happy when you called but did not think
anything of this sort could happen to us. For your
parents to be as kind to us as to one of their own
kin. Roselyn, how can you be grateful enough? It
seems that we are never financially able to do
anything for anyone, but maybe someday, some way,
we will get the opportunity to show our greatness.

Now, Roselyn, as far as Dave being in physical
danger, I really don't feel it is necessarily so.
I have a very strong feeling that Dave is being
disturbed emotionally. He won't go see a doctor. He
is trying to do too many things at one time. Some
of our people are fearful for him. They know that
his determination is strong so they fear, but not
enough to unite themselves because they are
fearful. When he gets home, he has been knocking
himself out such that there is no reasoning sense
with him at all, to the point where it has begun to
upset some of the children. I feel like I can be
honest with you people because you have proven
beyond a shadow of a doubt to be a friend to us.

Please, any advice or information you can pass on to us will be appreciated. I'm sure you know we feel the same about the Utzmans.

I'm going to give you an example of some of the things I am speaking of. Dave and I had an appointment with the guidance clinic on Thursday at 9 AM. We had it written down on the calendar. And, with Dave being disturbed, I was concerned about him and we both forgot the time and date. This was in regards to Avard. We knew how important this was, and yet we forgot it. Avard lost his hearing, so I took him to the hearing center, and they gave him tests and could not find anything wrong. It was just as I had thought. He was hearing things that he did not want to hear, so he began to ignore everything. I'm not writing this to disturb any of you. I just feel like maybe a friend's advice, if you have any, may help. All send love.

May God bless and keep us all,
The David Sims family

~~~~~~

Again, many points to address. Ruby references the kindness of Roselyn's parents in the first paragraph and hints at it being financial. To reveal the full extent of this most generous act would involve neutering the impact of Roselyn's next letter, so the subject shall be left as is for now.

As to the physical danger facing Mr. Sims, it is not clear if it stems from hostilities that those who wish him harm would inflict or if it is simply health-related, such as a stress-induced heart attack. Regardless, Ruby seems more concerned about her courageous crusader's emotional state and the effect it is having on some of the children. Mrs. Sims acknowledges that Roselyn, having demonstrated time and time again that their friendship is genuine, is someone she can confide in and appeal to for advice. The weight of being jobless for so long and now being prevented from working because of the strike, coupled with an impending foreclosure, must have been enormous. For Mr. Sims to hold up as well as he did, given such adverse circumstances, is a testament to his faith and fortitude. A lesser man would not have fared so well.

~~~~~~

Jan. 18, 1962
R.R. 3 Box 100
Spring Valley, Minn.

Dear David, Ruby, and children,

We plan to go to Spring Valley this afternoon, so I shall spend this morning getting some correspondence done. Then we can mail it in town.

When we were in the bank the other day, the banker gave us the enclosed loan form and we have filled it out. He said you folks would probably both sign it separately on the two bottom lines marked with the "X". My mom sent us the same kind of note to sign so you actually have borrowed the money from us. It grieved us to think of you folks losing your home, and as we discussed it and prayed about it, this seemed to be the answer. We pray that the difficulty at Studebaker will soon be straightened out so that men may have employment, homes, food, and security for their families.

We are enclosing the ticket drawn up at the bank. The $9.73 is what Western Union charged to send the money by wire. We hope this meets your approval.

The birthday book tells us that Cheryl, Fredonia, and Belinda are all celebrating birthdays this week. We want to enclose our greetings to them.

Yesterday, on Belinda's birthday, Leora (Debbie's mom) had a nice little girl calf. Debbie was named for the little girl whose birthday she was born on. Do you think Belinda would like this one named for her?

Mrs. Donald King, Geraldine, the lady who had Belinda one afternoon while you were here, underwent delicate heart surgery on Jan. 3rd and we rejoice that God has spared her life so that she can return to her family. The surgeons closed a hole in her heart the size of a half dollar and also did some other repair work.

We had Joyce to the doctor last Friday and he gave us the very happy news that Joyce could return to school this week. She is so happy to be going and thoroughly enjoys it. We thank you and your church for the prayers in her behalf. She is completely healed with no heart damage.

Now, our big project is preparing for our new baby. We are taking the hospital bed back this afternoon,

```
making room for the chest of drawers that was in
the bathroom upstairs to be brought down to put
baby's things in.
```

```
We hold you all in our thoughts and prayers and
hope that you will know the healing of a kind and
loving God as you continue on, day by day. We have
found such happy fellowship with you and your
community through Christ, who draws all men to
himself, and as we draw nearer to him, we become
closer to each other.
```

```
Our love to you all,
The Davids: Sharkey, Roselyn, Joyce, and Gregory
```

Well, the cat is out of the bag. Foreclosure on the Sims' property was stalled, thanks to a loan, officially from Marienus and Roselyn, but with money they borrowed from Roselyn's parents, Mr. and Mrs. Walter Attig, thus clarifying the reason for Ruby's gratitude, as mentioned in her previous letter. Mr. Sims echoes those sentiments in his next missive.

Two other notes of import: Mrs. Davids reveals that Joyce will return to school in a matter of days. That she is returning at all is in itself a minor miracle, let alone that she is doing so just four months after being stricken with this deadly disease. She was more of an observer at first, easing her way back into the curriculum and abiding by the doctor's orders not to engage in strenuous activity of any kind. But with the pronouncement that Joyce's heart suffered no damage, unheard of in a case so severe, it wasn't long before she was fully integrated back into the kindergarten program. Though she enjoyed it (at least according to her mother), Joyce struggled to keep up with her classmates academically, as the extended time away from school proved to be too much to overcome. Joyce would repeat kindergarten the following year, which turned out to be a blessing in disguise, as some of her dearest friends, even into adulthood, would be her classmates.

The family matriarch also gives some insight into the preparations for the arrival of Patricia Roselyn, the Davids' third bundle of joy, just ten days hence as of the heading's date. Joyce and Gregory were so excited at the time to welcome a new baby sister into the fold!

~~~~~~

Jan. 17, 1962
314 So. Ill. St.
So. Bend 19, Ind.

Mr. and Mrs. Davids,

Dearest friends - at this time, with a sigh of relief - thanks to God and you wonderful people, I can begin to think in terms of normal things. This past week has been exhausting for us. I was so worried, my mind preoccupied with the house and faced with a final exam. The effect of my inability to study showed up in my final grade in English – I got a 63. However, my semester average will give me a C. I'm sure that, even though I tried to shield my worry from Ruby, she was also distressed. Many things I have been told I dare not tell her simply because it would only serve to upset her even more.

I feel this is not the thing for me to do since she needs all the energy she can get to serve the children.

I took my problem to the Board of Directors of the Improvement Association, an organization with plans for a Savings and Loan Corporation. Being a member, I felt our plight warranted their consideration. After three hours of confused discussion, no action was taken on our behalf. However, three or four board members took a stand with me. This association has only four hundred members and $5000 in savings after two years of being in operation. Of course, certain members felt: here is a man who has financial difficulties trying to tell us what we should do. He evidently doesn't know how to manage his personal money; otherwise, he wouldn't be in this situation. Gentlemen, we know our aims; let's not waiver from our course until we reach our goal of $50,000 in savings. Only then do they feel they can even begin to do business. According to the present rate of pace of $5000 every two years, it will take this organization twenty years to accumulate $50,000.

Out of our family's plight, a new idea was born. The Homeowners Relief Corporation is in the process of being set up, with a subscription list presently being circulated. The law requires a $1000 minimum capital investment: ten men with $100 each or twenty men with $50 each. These men will be our officers. Attorney Wills can then proceed to get a charter

from the state, after which we will sell shares at
$10 per share. Our operation capital will also
consist of $50,000. However, our plans call for
immediate investment in properties, homes, cars,
etc., paying shareholders dividends from
accumulated profits. Our first project will be the
purchase of our home. The present owner agrees to
sell the property to the corporation at a 20%
discount if we can raise the balance by April 15,
1962. This means it is necessary for us to sell at
least 600 shares at $10/share by this date. If only
our people can see the need for this cooperative
enterprise, this will be the common interest that
can unite us all in a common cause. In short, it
will show our people, at a small cost to each of
us, that we have the power to collectively pool our
money to prevent the loss of home, car, furniture,
etc. and, at the same time, earn interest,
dividends, etc. The plan is fool-proof, legal,
and needed desperately by our people. If God be
with us, we can put this over. All who buy shares
in the corporation are automatically entitled to
equal benefits. They don't necessarily have to be
in my predicament: on the verge of eviction. The
basic idea is that if we as a people collectively
own our properties, it would be foolish to foreclose
during periods of distress. This will also unify
our people from all social classes into one economic
group. It can also be interracial, in as much as we
welcome the support of anyone who feels the
corporation warrants their support. We certainly

215

hope that other groups – real estate, banks, loan companies, etc. - don't stop us before we get started, as there isn't one financial loan buying and selling institution owned or operated by our people in South Bend today. But many are in operation. If we are successful, it will have some effect on their business since we will be competing with them for trade.

Please tell your wonderful parents we send a special word of prayer to them, to you folks, and to God. For without your immediate aid, I am certain the idea, as good as it was, would have been ignored. When you stated I would feel more confident appearing before those men, knowing all means of aid had not been exhausted, you were absolutely right. I stated to them, "Gentlemen, while you question my integrity, my thrift, indeed, my life's history, our friends in Minnesota have agreed to come to our aid without knowing anything about us, really. With or without your aid, Homeowner's Relief Corporation will be set up." At this time the president of the association said, "Go on with your idea, Mr. Sims. Put my name down for 20 shares." Three or four others said the same so, as you can see, it was only through your open hearts, faith in mankind, and love of God that brought all this about.

With all our love, prayers, and devotion,

David and Ruby Sims & family

P.S. Please forward all necessary papers in regards to the loan. Please include a life insurance policy so that, in the event of death, the loan will be paid. As soon as we get this corporation going, tell Marienus – of course, this goes for anyone – we want him to be a stockholder. Maybe he will need a new tractor. We can finance. Will write more later.

~~~~~~

Jan. 29, 1962
314 So. Ill. St.
So. Bend, Ind.

Dearest friends,

We pray these few lines find you in good health and spirits and that God will preserve your energy for the expected newborn. In spite of everything, our faith in God and his goodness will sustain us.

This a.m., we received a wonderful letter from Sharkey's brother expressing his concern and desire to share our burden as Christians. I can't tell you how grateful and appreciative we are to know God's goodness still prevails in the hearts of men. It is difficult to maintain faith in the human race when you are forced to deal daily with soulless men with an attitude of indifference and complete apathy. Human suffering means nothing to these people.

Did you, by any chance, see NBC White Paper's "The Newburgh Story"? This story was symbolic of the national plight of us all. I'm getting a letter of appreciation off to the studio for interest in human welfare shown by these people. Chet Huntley was the narrator.

Ruby, the children, and I hope and pray for your well-being. I must get a letter in the mail to Don Miller. As of yet, we haven't answered their correspondence. Also, we will reply to Mr. Davids. Whenever you are able to write again, there are many things we would like to discuss with you folks. In the meantime, our hopes and prayers to God will include the best for you and yours.

With all our love, prayers, and devotion.

Sincerely,
The Sims family

P.S. Thanks to all of you and God above for the loan. We will repay it as soon as possible.

~~~~~~

Most of the content of these two letters stands on its own and needs no further elaboration. That said, the reader is left to wonder about the Homeowner's Relief Corporation. Did it get established and sufficiently funded? Did it flourish? If so, were families like the Sims able to benefit from it? Sadly, there is no definitive answer to any of those questions. The corporation's prosperity would certainly warrant explication in future correspondence, yet Sims mentions the subject just once more and not in sufficient specificity such that reasonable conclusions can be drawn.

"The Newburgh Story" that Sims cites was a one-hour episode that aired on January 28, 1962, as part of NBC's "White Paper" documentary TV series. Narrated by the late great Chet Huntley, it focused on the town of Newburgh, New York and the efforts of its city manager, Joseph Mitchell, to reform the municipality's public assistance programs. At a press conference to announce his plan, Mitchell asserted, "Welfare has acted as a magnet to those who would immigrate into the city. It attracts the poor rather than repelling them."[39] Those immigrants, largely Black, were part of the Great Migration, in which African Americans had for decades been heading north, seeking higher-paying jobs and a better way of life. Lured in by promises of employment and cheap housing (which slum lords were all too eager to take advantage of), migrants discovered, due to various socioeconomic factors, a city in decline with few opportunities. Factories had closed and moved their operations south to take advantage of cheap labor.

A new highway bypassed the downtown area, causing many stores to close their doors. Many had no choice but to seek welfare benefits but would receive their checks only after a gestapo-style interrogation at police headquarters. As one recipient put it, Mitchell's war on welfare has made it "a crime to be poor."[40] Yet, only 11% of the city's welfare payments were dispersed to low-income families. The hard-hitting

---

[39] Joseph Mitchell (city manager). (2024, May 26). In Wikipedia. https://en.wikipedia.org/wiki/ Joseph_Mitchell_(city_manager)
[40] Riley, Shantal Paris. "Battle of Newburgh." Mid Hudson Times, April 2, 2013, https://www.timeshudsonvalley.com/mic-hudson-times/mid-hudson-times/stories/battle-of-newburgh,3131.

NBC expose uncovered that the remaining 89% was swallowed up by the city's infirmary for the elderly, which also housed blind and disabled individuals, as well as children in foster care.

Mitchell's scheme was originally viewed with optimism and was actually part of a broader movement – Urban Renewal – in which old, dilapidated commercial and residential areas were razed in favor of more modern businesses, apartment complexes, etc., designed to entice those who fled to suburbia and elsewhere back to the city. Ultimately, mounting opposition to Mitchell's tactics doomed his plan, and he resigned, but Urban Renewal continued, displacing hundreds of low-income residents.

"The longer I live, the better I know that there are no simple solutions to complicated problems," said former family court judge Edward O'Neill of Newburgh's difficulties. "Humanity and decency and morality are, in the long run, the only solutions to these problems or any other kinds of problems."[41]

---

[41] Riley, Shantal Paris. "Battle of Newburgh." Mid Hudson Times, April 2, 2013, https://www.timeshudsonvalley.com/mid-hudson-times/mid-hudson-times/stories/battle-of-newburgh,3131.

Chapter 17: Farewell, but Never Good-Bye

July 13, 1962
14 So. Illinois St.
South Bend, Indiana

Mr. & Mrs. Marienus Davids,

Dearest friends, maybe the enclosed literature will explain my long delay in responding about the hoped-for visit exchange this year. There was so much uncertainty; we simply could do nothing but hope and pray for the best. Unlike your pastor, leaving because his superiors sent him to do greater and more urgent work, our pastor, to a great extent, was forced to seek more Christian warmth due to a combination of things. There are many people in key positions in our church who do not display a Christian attitude. This, of course, makes it very difficult for a person to deal with or work with those who seem to get joy out of seeing the church program lag or fail. We have a lot of petty-minded people who seem to think that God's work is something to play with. Our pastor's departure to Kansas City, Missouri, is one of the most tragic things that could have happened, not only to the church but to the community as well. I'm sure most people feel the same way as we do about their pastor but believe me when I say, our pastor was and remains an exceptionally outstanding minister, and not just in the community or the state. We rank him among the best in the nation. If given an appreciative audience and just a few good, intelligent people to work with, our minister could and would perform miracles, be it God's will.

I am enclosing a partial payment of annual interest on the loan. We were relieved that you folks gave us the opportunity to start payments next year. We will be able to pay a lump sum after income tax time. I recall you mentioning that you may be without the Utzmans. We have had a similar experience and fully realize your mixed emotions. Maybe it is wrong for us to say that we hated to see our minister go to a better place. Maybe it is selfishness on our part, but when you have spent years of comradeship, divine love, and close worshipping together with someone, parting isn't easy.

Also, we're forwarding the package for the baby this time. Carla mailed my other letter without my knowledge, not knowing it was my intention to send the package at that time.

Ruby and the children all send their love. Carla received an invitation to spend a few weeks' vacation with Emilie Snyder. We were thrilled to know this was the desire of both Emilie and her parents. However, at this time, it would be impossible for Carla to come as she is working on the farm to aid our income, along with Paul, Cheryl, and Fredonya. They earn two to three dollars per day. Sometimes, this helps them buy a few things that, otherwise, we could not afford.

Again, we ask that you extend our love to the entire community. Our pastor expressed his regrets that the visit could not materialize due to the circumstances. He would have been happy to have such a visit under his leadership.

We desire the prayers of everyone during these difficult times. We need all the aid we can get in hopes of weathering this storm of disunity and strife in the house of God.

Each of us sends our love to you and yours.

Sincerely yours,
David and Ruby Sims & children

~~~~~~

What should immediately stand out to the reader is the date of this letter. Five and one-half months have passed since last Mr. Sims put pen to paper. He hopes the "enclosed literature" will explain the delay, but the nature of that literature is unclear. That said, if one is to postulate, it might very well have something to do with the minister of the church the Sims attend departing for greener pastures. It is obvious, at least to Mr. Sims, why he is leaving. Whether it was his choice to seek a new parish or that choice was made for him, it would appear that it resulted from the action of church officials who cared more about politics and power than the principles of the gospel. Needless to say, the Sims adore their pastor and are devastated by this loss, as exemplified by the profusion of praise heaped upon this godly man by the Sims patriarch. This debacle, coupled with some of the children working the strawberry farms to supplement the family income, seems to have put the kibosh on any plans for a visit exchange in the summer of '62.

Content from the first two paragraphs indicates that Mr. Sims is somehow aware that the Sumner Center church may also be losing its beloved pastor, Reverend Utzman, although under different circumstances. This knowledge may have resulted from a phone conversation or a snippet in one of Roselyn's as-of-yet-undiscovered letters. In fact, it saddens this author to reveal that the letter dated January 18 is the Davids' matriarch's last. Others certainly exist (or existed) as Sims alludes to information in them and will continue to do so. If tucked away in the aforementioned shoebox, perhaps, someday, they will see the light of day. If they have, instead, been sucked into the abyss normally reserved for TV remotes and socks from the dryer, Roselyn's pearls of wisdom and sage advice shall, unfortunately, forever be lost to present and future generations. Of course, another explanation, albeit remote, is that Roselyn stopped creating duplicate copies of the letters she wrote to the Sims. The reasoning behind such a decision remains allusive, nor is there any evidence to support such a hypothesis. If only Nancy Drew or the Hardy Boys could be summoned to solve the mystery of the missing missives.

~~~~~~

To our beloved pastor, the Reverend Mr. F. W. Johnson

By Sunday School Branch

Farewell but never Good-bye.

On behalf of the Sunday School, and as superintendent of that branch of this church, it is my desire to express the sentiments of those who love you.

Reverend Johnson: as our friend, as our dedicated and devoted leader, as one who has given much love and kindness, as one who has sacrificed both time and energy, and, above all, as one who is a child of God, we say to you, dear pastor, "Farewell, but never Good-bye."

Realizing the penalties a leader must suffer needlessly and, on many occasions, unjustly, the Christian experience has taught us that only a child of God could suffer the many abuses you, as our leader, have suffered and still have love in your heart for us.

On many occasions, for your extended love and kindness, you, as our beloved pastor, were rebuked and scorned, your outstretched arms of friendship were bypassed, your divine council was rejected, and your inspired sermons fell on deaf ears. Yes, the time and energy you so willingly gave was not appreciated by those of us who did not have God in our hearts.

However, our beloved pastor, for those of us who do have the love of God and our fellow man in our hearts, we pray to God and ask your forgiveness for any and all wrongs and injustices you have suffered during your eleven-year stay among this flock.

We consider it proper and fitting at this time to say to you that, among this flock, there are those who do appreciate your dedicated and devoted service, your undying love, your radiant smile, your tears of joy and grief, your sincere spiritual guidance, your divinely inspired sermons, your words of consolation during times of grief, and the many sleepless nights you spent praying about all of our problems. Yes, beloved pastor, you were the good shepherd of this flock.

The remoteness of time and space cannot separate us from the good seeds you have sown in this community, this state, and throughout the nation.

We are sure you know your words and deeds shall always remain with us and inspire us further to seek God and his righteousness. Your humility in the face of arrogance, your love in the face of contempt, your silence in the face of lies, and your compassion in the face of anger are all qualities of the Christian virtues that your life exemplified. These qualities will be treasured by each of us. Yes, your influence in this community will be felt for generations to come.

May you find consolation to add to your inner peace when we say thanks for a job well done.

It is difficult for us to say farewell at this time; however, our hearts tell us that we'd rather see you go where there is more happiness, more love, more appreciation, more devotion, more concern,

indeed, more Christian warmth. This, we feel, you
have earned and so richly deserve.

Our love is not a selfish one. We'd rather give you
up than keep you from a greater blessing if it be
God's will. Our prayers go with you. May God keep
and preserve you. May he ever watch over you. May
he guide and protect you. May he ever bless you for
the betterment of this nation. Yes, our beloved
pastor, New Salem, says to you, "farewell, but never
good-bye."

Though unsigned, the style and verbiage of this letter scream David
Sims. It seems to have been written on behalf of the church's adult
Sunday School class and reflects their sentiments and,
undoubtedly, those of many other church members. The dates of
the writing of the letter, as well as the disconsolate occasion of
Reverend Johnson's departure, remain nebulous, but one thing is
crystal clear: Reverend Johnson was dearly loved and will be sorely
missed by a good portion of the congregation of New Salem Baptist
Church.

August 4, 1962
314 So. Illinois St.
South Bend, Indiana

Mr. and Mrs. Marienus Davids,

Dearest friends, we hope and pray everything is well with you. We have been somewhat disturbed by our lack of communication with you folks. Forgive the intrusion of this letter for it may arrive at a time when you least need be disturbed. It is our desire to know if you are well and if everything is well with you since you last wrote.

We will not go into any lengthy discussion in this letter about anything other than to say we are enclosing a "JET" in case you haven't had the chance to see this issue.

Our hearts were thrilled to read the story. Who knows how many such stories go unpublished or unheard of nationally throughout the land.

The Catholic Interracial Council (CIC) was organized a year ago. They are doing a great job in conjunction with the Urban League.

Ruby asked me to express her gratitude for "The World Evangel". It is quite informative and we enjoy the reading material in it.

How are your folks in Iowa? Each time we write, we assume you express our equal concern about their welfare, also.

The children all send love and often ask why we did not remain there in your area. Carla recently received a letter from Emilie Snyder. Someone put it away and, as of yet, we haven't been able to find it. The smaller children often handle the mail. David and Harold both attended summer school. David failed English 1 during the regular term. He managed to get a "C" this time. Harold was working for extra credits; however, we don't know if he will receive any or not since he failed to make up a test. At the time, we were not familiar with summer school rules, so he did not get a report card (any test missed = course flunked).

Did you receive the token gift for the baby? Have you folks been on vacation this year? How are the crops this year? Have you been able to visit with the Utzmans yet? How are your folks in Villa Park? How is Spring Valley?

We are enclosing the remainder of this year's interest on the loan. Economic conditions haven't been in our favor at all this year. This four-day workweek only pays our food bill.

Here's hoping and praying everything is alright with all of you.

All our love,
Ruby, David, and family

~~~~~~

Several statements and questions are to be addressed in this letter, foremost of which is the concern on the part of the Sims that communication between the two families has been less than ideal of late. While it is reasonable to assume that the January 18th letter sent by Mrs. Davids is not actually the most recent one, enough time has elapsed since she last wrote so as to be unsettling. The angst on the part of the Sims is the result of genuine affection for their friends and a sincere hope that everything is alright with them.

The Jet magazine issue referred to is probably not the previously mentioned one, as it was over a year old by this time. As this is the first time Mr. Sims mentions the CIC, one might conclude that the Jet magazine issue probably contains an article about this organization, but attempts to research previous issues online that contained such information proved fruitless. That said, it is worth mentioning that the Catholic Interracial Council of New York was created in 1934 as a way for White and Black Catholics to come together to fight racial injustice. It expanded into other cities, and the Chicago chapter, in particular, grew to prominence in the 1950s, helping to de-escalate racial tensions that erupted in certain areas of the country. This led to the creation, in 1961, of the National Catholic Conference of Interracial Justice. The NCCIJ coordinated the efforts of the CICs in New York, Chicago, and elsewhere, serving as a civil rights advocacy arm that worked with other like-minded organizations such as the Urban League.

"The World Evangel" Ruby expresses gratitude for was a monthly magazine published in the 1960s by the Women's Society of World Service of the EUB church. Its article content dealt with a variety of topics related to Christianity, including missionary work, human interest stories, and tips on day-to-day living. The EUB church merged with the Methodist Church to form the United Methodist Church (UMC) in 1968, effectively ending the magazine's publication.

Most of the questions in paragraph eight cannot be answered without further correspondence from Mrs. Davids, but the question regarding Rev. Utzman suggests that he has already moved on. He was succeeded by Rev. Howard Mueller, who took the reins sometime during the summer of 1962 and baptized Patricia on August 12th. He served as the church pastor until 1965.

The next letter in this collection of communiqués is dated January 27, 1963. What transpired in the lives of the Davids and Sims family members during the five-month letter hiatus is purely conjecture. One would assume that the two families at least exchanged Christmas cards, but that, too, is unverified. What is known is that Joyce, who turned six in August, returned to school in the fall to begin again her kindergarten experience. Greg, still too young to attend school, remained at home with baby sister Patricia, who would turn one year old in January of 1963. Sharkey continued his farming ways while Roselyn stayed busy taking care of the "youngins", cooking, teaching piano lessons, and the occasional speaking engagement.

While the Sims family members appear to be in good health and spirits, one can't help but wonder just how much the children questioned their father's decision to return to South Bend. Mr. Sims made this decision based on what would keep his family safe, and given the racial strife of that decade, coupled with the death threats they received, who could blame him? Regardless, their financial situation, despite the loan, remains grim, as does the prospect of long-term employment, which Sims will elaborate on in the next two letters.

Chapter 18: On Again, Off Again

January 27, 1963
314 So. Illinois St.
South Bend 19, Indiana

Dearest friends,

You will never realize what your faith, confidence, patience, and forbearance have meant in our lives. Trust, such as you have displayed in our friendship, is beyond comprehension. When our friends and associates are told of your heartfelt act of kindness and concern, they marvel in awe.

It appears that each time I'm supposed to begin my payments, something crops up and necessitates a delay. I was laid off on January 2nd from S.P. Corporation. However, I was fortunate enough to secure employment with the city again on Friday, January 25th. There is only one disadvantage here. I would prefer employment in private industry since our city government is the most corruptible element in our society. I don't appreciate the stigma attached to the job. First, one must be a Democrat and vote the Democrat ticket. Second, one must work at the polls for said Democrat candidate during election time. However, in my case, as in many others, I have no choice. Either I accept this offer of employment or be doomed to the relief rolls until S.P. calls me back or other employment becomes available. Only God knows when that day will come, and, of course, "survival" will not permit us time to wait and see.

It was my intention to make my first payment on the 15th of this month. Loss of employment necessitates a delay... until now. As long as I have this job, you can expect payments to be mailed on the 25th of each month, as this job pays twice monthly, on the 5th and the 25th.

Grandma Hunter stated that your sister had her baby. We pray they are both well as, of course, the rest of the family. We've wondered if you were able to visit her and why no reply as to whether or not you would be able to visit our home. Was our response too late in reaching you? Did you receive our letter of reply? We hope you folks take it for granted that our doors shall forever remain open to you and you have a permanent invitation at all times.

The winter has been pretty severe here. 0-degree temperatures have been with us for quite some time. Our church obligations have kept us quite busy. Our new pastor is from Detroit. His name is Rev. L.C. Swan. We are in the process of raising funds for bricks. The drive ends the second week in February. I'm afraid I will not be able to keep my pledge under the circumstances.

I am enclosing our personal check for the month of January because it costs less than a money order. If this poses any problem for you folks, let us know, and we will convert it back to the money order. We hope to see you folks this year some way, somehow. This semester, I fell down horribly on my grades. Due to a biology requirement, I didn't have time to devote to my other studies, so I got a D in Math and Business English. This semester, I am taking Business Math I over again. I know I am capable of doing the work. I managed to get a C in Biology I. I felt after getting into it that Biology was more important than the other two subjects, so most of my study time, notebook keeping, etc. was devoted to that subject. Everything about the subject depended on memory. On our final exam, we had 172 questions. I answered 121 correctly. This, along with my test average, only rated me a C.

There is a good possibility of us getting a mortgage loan on our home and reducing our payment by $7 a month if things work out for us.

Ruby and the children all send their love. Say hello to everyone for us. A special hello to Patricia, Joyce, and Greg from the children. We desire to hear from you at the earliest convenience.

Love from all,
Ruby and David Sims & family

~~~~~~

As a man of honor and integrity, David Sims is obviously deeply troubled that he cannot keep his word regarding the loan repayment plan as originally agreed upon. After losing one job but securing another (despite its egregious requirements), he hopes this month's remittance will be the start of regular installments. Sims offers prayers for Roselyn's sister and her new baby and wonders why a swing over to South Bend for a visit wasn't in the cards. Of course, he is referring to Marilyn Miller, Roselyn's one and only sibling, who resides in Villa Park, Illinois. The new baby, Kenny, is one of six children. This is worthy of mention because tragedy would strike six years later, as Kenny would lose his life in a car-pedestrian accident, a loss that devastated the family. As to why the Davids did not continue on to South Bend or communicate their plans to the Sims, that is open to speculation, as are so many things without Roselyn's correspondence.

One final point: the mortgage loan. Was it ever secured? Not likely, as it is never mentioned again in any of Mr. Sims' letters. One would surmise that the topic would be broached in subsequent correspondence if David and Ruby's application was approved.

~~~~~~

February 24, 1963
314 So. Illinois St.
South Bend 19, Indiana

Mr. and Mrs. Marienus Davids,

Dearest friends, it appears I will not be able to keep my word again due to unemployment again. I might have known I could place no confidence in the words of corrupt officials. The city government again raised my hopes for steady employment and let me down again, as they did right after my return from our visit with you folks.

You recall my short period of employment with school

235

city, which was brought on by a lot of trees in our area being infected with "Dutch Elm Disease." The city needed a crew of temporary help to meet the emergency, permitting those hired to think permanent employment would follow if their work proved out to the city's satisfaction. When the bulk of the heavy work was done, we got the boot.

A similar "emergency" existed as a result of our recent snowstorm. Now that this emergency is over – a temp working in the removal of snow and ice – it appears, in fact, I have been informed by Mr. Richardson, our street commissioner, that as of February 28th, my services will no longer be needed. You can understand the hollow of insecurity I feel. Even though the pay was 98 cents per hour less than what I earned at S.P. Corporation and the work consisted of nine hr days (a 45-hour work week), I was extremely grateful to have what I thought was steady employment.

As a result, due to absolute necessity, and because my unemployment compensation claim is exhausted until June, I must drop my studies for the rest of this semester and take a flight to another city to seek employment. As yet, I will be forced to remain here until March 5th to get my pay, so I will have a few funds to use for travel expenses. I've heard there is a chance for temporary employment in the East Chicago area in the steel mill. They are stockpiling steel now in preparation for an anticipated strike before the 1964 negotiations begin.

A fellow has informed me — in fact, several have said — that the company is hiring, and they usually permit employees to work from 60 to 80 days before discharging them. At 90 days, one would be eligible for union membership and, of course, they don't like this. I will be grateful for any amount of days or weeks of gainful employment under the circumstances.

We hope everyone is doing fine. As always, we send our best wishes to you. If we even have half a chance, it is our intention to some way, somehow try and succeed in securing a stable, lasting income (if such a thing exists). Once this on-again-off-again income business is out of the way, I can maybe settle down to being a half-normal human being. As always, or in most cases, our letters to you are distressing, this I realize. The intent is not to distress but to keep you informed as to how things really are with us, not for sympathy or charity but for clear understanding.

Our friends informed us that our visit was mentioned on the local TV station. We didn't hear or see it, as our set has been out of operation since Christmas. We look forward to a brighter day with hope of a cherished love that the understanding, patience, and forbearance you folks have shown us can someday soon be repaid in deeds as well as words.

I live in constant agony, realizing that no matter how hard I try – always when it comes time for action – some unseen incident defies my innermost desire to be able to keep my word. All I can do for now is to appeal to Marienus and you to keep the faith with me. I am determined to prove worthy of the trust you placed in me. Somehow, I must come through, and with God's aid, I will.

Everyone sends love to each of you. We'll write again. As soon as adjustments can be made, money will be forthcoming.

Sincerely and with all our love,
David & Ruby Sims and family

~~~~~~

It seems Mr. Sims can't catch a break. He wants desperately to provide adequately for his wife and children, yet forces beyond his control stifle his every effort. Nonetheless, his faith remains strong and he presses forward, determined to find the kind of long-term employment that will allow him to not only feed his family but, as a man of integrity, make good on his loan agreement with the Davids.

As for the reference to "our visit," it is likely the Sims' week-long excursion to the Davids' farm, as the only other "visit" since would have been the foursome's pilgrimage to Dayton for the NUL conference. Why either of these two events would have made TV news so many months later is uncertain.

314 So. Illinois St.
South Bend, Indiana
April 10, 1963

Dearest friends,

Today, as you know, is our eighteenth wedding anniversary. We were elated to receive your heartwarming letter. As always, we are without words to describe our innermost feelings for your open hearts. We can only pray for God's preservation for people such as yourselves, who are priceless jewels. We draw strength from your patience, endurance, and kindness.

How my heart bleeds each time we write. I must share grievous news with you folks. You recall my going to Chicago to seek work. I ran down several ads that stated "equal opportunity employer", thinking that if I am qualified for the job, at least I stand a chance of being hired. At Inland Steel, I was told I had to have a high school diploma to sweep the floor. At International Harvesters, "We will check with Studebakers." At Vapor Corporation, "We'll call you."

All this, I took in stride. However, the most grievous one – the one that hurt me the most – was Chicago Transit Authority.

Here at this company, applicants are required to take a written test even before the company considers your application for employment. If one flunks the test, the process is stopped to eliminate hiring costs. I passed the test, passed the physical

239

exam, and was fingerprinted. I was told my police and work records were sent out for investigation. Today, I called and was told my application was rejected. They will not reveal why. I'm sure you know how I feel, having passed the written test and the physical; yet, there are shadows in my background that prevent me from earning a living for my family – shadows that my potential employer will never reveal to me. One would think that if, in the past, I had made a mistake, they would reveal it to me. I would then try to correct it, but they will not tell me why they can't hire me. I can't do anything but wonder. I have no serious criminal record, and I have worked during my lifetime, in most cases, for as long as the employer permitted me to. To me, it just doesn't add up. I tell you this: insecurity is definitely taking its toll on Ruby and the family. We'll talk about this and other things after you arrive.

Just now, we would like to know if you would arrive on the 20th of April early, as we would like to arrange for you to meet some of the people in our community. If you can plan to spend Sunday the 21st here also, you would be able to meet some other people in the Catholic Interracial Council, a group trying to get restricted housing open to our people. I have attended several of their meetings. I'm not too popular with this group because I have been urging them to direct their attention to more urgent matters needed by our people. I will explain to you folks when we meet. Please answer as soon as possible, as our plans depend entirely upon the time that you will be available. Believe me, our community stands to gain much in an educational way. It should be quite interesting to see what kind of "community hospitality response" will be given to you, inasmuch as our family was so well received by your community. You can believe me when I say we have a lot of hypocrites in key positions in our city, both Negro and White. I will keep you folks posted as to who is who. I am certain you will keep it quiet.

This is all for now – answer soon.

Love from all,
Ruby, David, and family

P.S. Invitations can't be mailed until we know your arrival date. This will not be a real big thing, but very educational, I promise you.

~~~~~~

Note that almost two months have passed since Mr. Sims' previous epistle, understandable as he ventured out of the confines of South Bend and into the morass that was Chicago, seeking that elusive, steady, full-time job. Sadly, his efforts were in vain, as he painfully recounted, incredulous as to how the Chicago Transit Authority could deny employment without specifying why, especially since he had passed the physical and written tests. He legitimately wondered what black mark(s) (likely bogus) could be on his record that would prompt such a decision. Given his outspokenness on race-related issues, might his record have been purposely tainted to curtail employment and if so, by whom? Though sounding conspiratorial, such queries seem reasonable, given Sims' past experiences.

On a positive note, it sounds as if the two families will be providing a sequel of sorts to their get-together from two summers ago, this time in South Bend.

The Sims – as well as their neighbors – are seemingly anxious to show the Davids the same kind of hospitality they were shown while visiting the homestead of their Sumner Center friends some 21 months previous. Sims is hopeful for a positive community response but mindful that local hypocrites in high places may be unsupportive of the planned reunion, which could manifest disharmony.

Chapter 19: Hoosier Hospitality

Did the highly anticipated summer-of-'62 redux come to fruition? Indeed, it did! Kudos to the South Bend Tribune for covering it in such great detail! While other newspapers contained nary a brief blurb about the splendid stay, the Tribune's article was replete with sufficient items of interest to adequately portray the happenings of that eventful weekend.

The South Bend sojourn actually began with a letter written to the Sims two weeks earlier by Roselyn (one of the many missing missives) informing them that after a Friday night stay at the Millers in Villa Park, Marienus, Roselyn, Joyce, Gregory, and baby Patricia would leave the Chicago area early Saturday a.m. and arrive in South Bend later that morning. In a later interview, Ruby beamed as she excitedly recounted the anticipation. "I was thrilled at the idea of seeing Roselyn again."[42]

The ardent adventurers did, in fact, arrive at the Sims' humble abode on the morning of April 20th. After warm greetings from the Sims, the Davids were treated to a hearty breakfast, much of which was supplied by friends and neighbors, who stopped by throughout the morning with donations – food and otherwise – to assist the Sims in entertaining their guests. Many simply wanted to meet the Davids, as previous press coverage had made them celebrities of sorts in this

---

[42] Field, Kenneth. "Farm Family Gets Taste of City Hospitality." The South Bend Tribune, April 21, 1963, p.38.

close-knit community.

The afternoon was filled with sightseeing, courtesy of the Catholic Interracial Council of South Bend. As the children stayed behind to play games and swap stories, Sharkey and Roselyn hobnobbed with the members of this and other organizations dedicated to improving relations between Blacks and Whites and discussed ways of making today's occurrence commonplace among them.

The delightful day culminated with dinner at the home of Ruby's aunt, Mrs. Dora Lottie, who had petitioned her niece to host the revered visitors, as she was unable to meet with them during their previous visit. The food was scrumptious, the conversation lively, as the attendees regaled one another with tales of how their lives had changed since that first letter Mrs. Davids mailed to KROC Rochester back in 1959. Of course, they also included the almost inexhaustible exploits of their offspring, leading Roselyn to comment, "Ruby and I have children, and our problems are the same. It's that simple." Mrs. Davids went on to declare, "I'm really having a nice time. The difference in our pigmentation doesn't seem like much of a barrier."[43]

Before heading home on Sunday, the Davids were honored guests at the New Salem Baptist Church for a very special service of prayer and fellowship. Both the Davids and Sims were recognized for their efforts in promoting and demonstrating the kind of unbridled Christian love that can go a long way toward tearing down barriers

---

[43] Field, Kenneth. "Farm Family Gets Taste of City Hospitality." The South Bend Tribune, April 21, 1963, p.38.

erected by those who would keep the races at odds.

Neither the Sims nor Davids siblings remember much about this event-filled weekend, but Greg, who was only four years old at the time, does recall a couple of interesting aspects of the church service. As is customary for many denominations, plates were passed for an offering after the sermon. What little Gregory found unusual was what came next. The offering plates were brought to the pastor, who, upon examining the contents, replied, "Well, that's just not enough!" The ushers were shooed back into the congregation and collected what were deemed to be satisfactory donations. After the service, everyone gathered in the basement fellowship hall to munch on popcorn (which Greg very much enjoyed) and visit with this fabled white family from Minnesota that they had heard so much about.

As the Davids headed back to Minnesota, both families undoubtedly reflected on what had been an absolutely wonderful weekend. Were the Sims successful in reciprocating the hospitality shown to them by the Sumner community? It would appear so, as according to Roselyn, "Everyone is so kind and friendly. The Sims are our kind of people."[44]

This photograph accompanied the aforementioned Tribune article. While all of the Davids are present, two of the Sims' children (David III and Harold) were not at home during its taking. From left to right in the back: Ruby, Roselyn, Aunt Vivian Scott (Ruby's sister), Charlotte, Michael Maddox (Vivian's son), Paul (holding the Sims'

---

[44] Field, Kenneth. "Farm Family Gets Taste of City Hospitality." The South Bend Tribune, April 21, 1963, p.38.

dog, Midnight), and Carla Diane. From left to right in front:

Freda, Joyce, Cheryl, Belinda, Gregory, Marienus (with baby Patricia on his lap), and David (with Avard seated in front of him). Whatever Gregory is doing, Avard and Cheryl seem amused by it. Notice that Paul is the only person who is both smiling and looking directly at the camera. This may be intentional, or perhaps the photographer forgot to ask everyone to "look at me and say cheese."

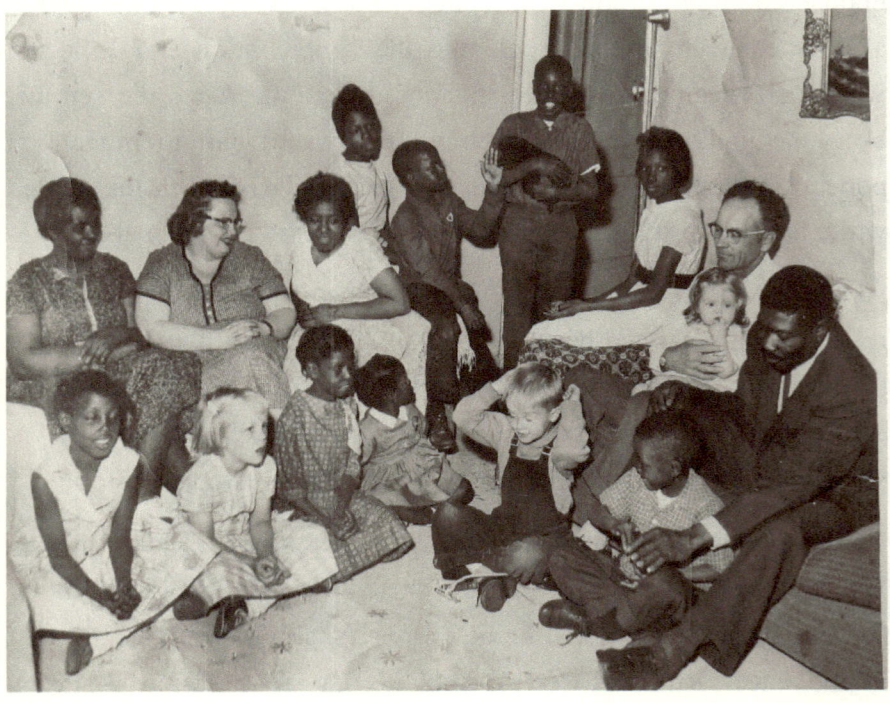

Circumstances on both sides would make it increasingly difficult to rendezvous again. Life on a dairy farm is all-consuming: the land is plowed, the crops are sown and eventually harvested, pigs are fattened up and sold for slaughter, and then there are the cows, which must be milked twice a day every day. Later that year, Marienus and Roselyn would fly to Korea to pick up and formally adopt the previously mentioned Jonathan and Maureen. Now, with five children, ages two to seven years old, it is easy to see how the Davids' vacation time would be extremely limited.

As for the Sims, the strain of caring for a wife and nine children, all while going to school and searching for steady employment, was taking its toll on the passionate patriarch, as the messaging in his missives will continue to bear out. Without Roselyn's half of the correspondence, the story is certainly less captivating; however, David Sims, ever the wordsmith and tale-teller, more than compensates by engaging the reader with wit and candor as he denounces the racism he sees and experiences first-hand. Certain battles may be over, but the war has just begun.

Chapter 20: Battles Fought; Solutions Sought

May 29, 1963
314 So. Illinois St.
South Bend 19, Indiana

Dearest friends,

Since we last met, much has transpired that has kept Ruby and I preoccupied. Ruby has secured a few days of work caring for children, and I was fortunate enough to be one of 25 trainees selected out of a group of 256 applicants for the Manpower Development Training Act. This, as you know, is a federal support plan to retrain unemployed heads of households, school drop-outs, etc. A course in general machine operation is presently being offered. We get 8 hours of schooling 5 days a week for 48 weeks. As you can see, this is indeed a genuine effort on the part of the federal government – with local cooperation – to do something about massive and chronic unemployment. As one of the recipients, I can't be grateful enough for this once-in-a-lifetime golden opportunity. We are receiving $33/month in support money, along with a basic course in arithmetic, algebra, geometry, trigonometry, etc. Also included is an additional course in blueprint reading, plus practical application in the school's machine shop.

As you can see, this is the real McCoy, and I don't have time to do too much of anything but study if

I am to maintain a passing grade. Domestic difficulties pose serious problems but we accept the challenge gladly. As always, extend our love to the people of your community and our desire to someday visit your area again. Our people asked us to express wishes of well-being and the best for you and yours. As to our business adventure, we have been able to secure a van; however, this unit cost left us without funds to secure other necessary equipment, license, etc. We are making progress, slow but sure. If things continue to go well with us, maybe by the end of the year, we will have secured enough funds to get started. At least, this is our hope and desire.

You must prevail upon Rev. Utzman and the Millers in particular – we are not ignoring their letters in the least. It is just that we never seem to have the time to adequately correspond with them as we desire due to the constant, pressing problems. Tell them it is our desire to make up for this as soon as we get our heads above the economic drowning point in this swim for survival. Tell all of your folks hello. We wish them well and, as soon as possible, money will be forthcoming. We are enclosing our only copy I managed to get from the Tribune. Ruby suggested you could have yourselves a print made from this and return it if this be your desire. Will you kindly copy the words from the poem "Negro Mother" and forward it to me at your earliest convenience as my church secretary

misplaced my only copy. I would appreciate it to
the highest.

As always, everyone sends their best in love and
devotion to our lasting goodwill and friendship.
Many things we desire to say, due to space and time,
we must forgo for the time being. We desire to hear
from you at your convenience.

Sincerely,
Ruby and David Sims & family

~~~~~~

Game-changing news from Mr. Sims as he relates, with renewed vigor, his induction into a government-sponsored program that could translate into full-time employment once completed. The training and education received should prepare him for a myriad of blue-collar jobs, any of which would be a vast improvement over his current situation. One cannot help but admire his can-do attitude and strength of spirit, especially in the face of such adversity.

The Tribune article is most likely the one quoted from in the previous chapter.

The poem "The Negro Mother" was referenced earlier as the poem Ruby may have read at the Mother's Day church service and appears to have meant a great deal to Mr. Sims. It was written and published in 1931 by Langston Hughes, an accomplished American poet, novelist, playwright, and columnist. Hughes is considered one of the earliest innovators of the literary art form called jazz poetry and is best known as a leader in the "Harlem Resistance", a rebirth of African American art, music, dance, literature, and fashion that occurred during the 1920s and 1930s. Centered in Harlem, New York, the final destination of countless Negroes fleeing oppressive conditions in the South, the movement's influence was felt around the country and even as far away as Paris, France, which was, at that time, home to many transplanted Black authors from Africa and the Caribbean. Originally known as "The New Negro Movement", it reached its zenith in the late 1920s but was severely curtailed by the stock market crash of 1929.

Langston Hughes was of mixed descent, as paternal and maternal ancestors included both slaves and slave owners. After his parents divorced, he was raised by his maternal grandmother, who instilled in him a great sense of pride in his heritage and empathy for the Negro plight in America. He wrote of such in his poetry, short stories, plays, and, after becoming more involved in social activism, a weekly column, which he penned for *The Chicago Defender,* a national publication that advocated for civil rights.[45]

"The Negro Mother" is a touching tale of a strong Black woman who endured the typical hardships associated with slavery. Despite such wretchedness, she persevered, knowing that her fight for freedom and equality for her people might not manifest for her but would for her descendants. Her strength and resilience are a testament to a mother's undying love for her "children."

---

[45] Langston Hughes. (2024, December 21). In *Wikipedia.* https://en.wikipedia.org/ wiki/Langston_Hughes

Permission was not granted to reprint the poem here. However, as previously mentioned, a Google search can easily produce a copy of "The Negro Mother." Time with her would be well-spent.

~~~~~~

July 13, 1963
314 So. Illinois St.
South Bend 19, Indiana

Dearest friends,

We hope and pray everyone is well in hope and spirit. As always, we look forward to your wonderful, heartwarming, and encouraging letters. You will never know what it means to us to know that we have sincere and dedicated friends and allies during these perilous times as we struggle, hope, trust, and pray for an extension of democracy (complete, unabridged freedom).

It is very difficult for me to understand what our nation has to fear from such an overdue act of simple humanity. For in reality, the inhumane and brutal suffering that our population has endured during the past generation, compounded with today's needless suffering and strife, forces our people to pay triple indemnity for a freedom that has indeed been bought and paid for in advance.

The worst part of our tragedy — the thing that has in the past and currently retards our struggle for freedom — is the lack of history about our people in this land. Your people, as well as many of our own, know absolutely nothing about the terrific struggle and sacrifices our people have made to keep the spark of freedom alive against tremendous odds. Not to mention the various contributions made by our people through their labor in this country in every field of endeavor. As a result of this lack of knowledge, many of your people and my own feel that – in their own words – "Negroes are demanding on a silver platter what others previously fought and died for." Devoid of our history, what else could they think?

For many years, our people have asked the nation's educators to include Negro history and our people's contributions to the development and maintenance of this nation. As yet, this plea is still ignored.

Yes, Dr. King is doing a wonderful job for America, but what this nation needs is ten thousand Dr. Kings. The apathy and general lack of concern among the leading class of your people and petty, bourgeoisie Negroes in key positions in our society has hampered and retarded the struggle in general. You would be surprised how disorganized and unconcerned the Negro ministry, the Urban League, the local chapter of the N.A.A.C.P., and all of the Negroes who are supposed to provide mass leadership for our people actually feel. In our people's language, they act and think white. According to their standards, every Negro must have a PhD from Harvard before he is qualified for a job. Since 1961, out of all the league's efforts, they have only been able to secure 65 jobs for our people. With 93% of all relief recipients being our people, you'll understand what I mean. The only time the local branch can do anything is when one's civil rights have been violated, such as refused service in a restaurant, etc. What I am attempting to say is that these people do not feel the pulse of the masses they are supposed to represent. They have no mass program past experience on a local level, which has taught us they do not have mass interest at heart. If concern isn't shown within the near future, the masses will and must act. Our pitiful plight demands this action.

Upon the recommendation of the president and the governor of our state, a biracial committee has been set up to study discrimination in employment, housing, and education. We pray that honesty, sincerity, and a desire to remove this evil prevails. We have found those selected to serve on the committee are mostly the same people who, in the past, have proven to have little or no regard for the effects of racial discrimination on our people. For example, Stanley G. Ladd, president of the Union Council, is well aware of discrimination in the unions in our area. We seriously doubt his desire to expose discrimination in the very organization he heads. The same goes for the executives of Studebaker Corporation, Bendix, the Realty Corp., etc.

The Negroes who were selected to serve, with few exceptions, are petty, bourgeoisie Negroes; that is, those who enjoy a margin of security in jobs and have decent homes. They refer to themselves as moderates. In our peoples' language, these are the type of Negroes that are content with self-preservation only and couldn't care less about the welfare of their downtrodden brothers.

So, you see that our people are confronted with a tremendous task. We will have to fight hard to get the committee to function, for, in reality, we have a committee composed, in part, of Negroes who are interested in personal gain and self-aggrandizement at the expense of our people's lives.

I wrote a poem as a tribute to Medgar Evers. I'll send it next time we write.

As always, our sincere love,
Ruby & David Sims and family

This Sims' epistle marks a departure from family news in favor of railing against racism, as the subject matter and tenor are more akin to a letter one would read in the local paper's editorial section. For better or worse, subsequent letters, for the most part, follow suit. Notice there is not one mention of any Sims family member. It would appear that the charismatic crusader's passion for righting wrongs pertaining to the treatment of "his people" consumed him more and more, which, in turn, spurred him to action. Case in point: the Medgar

Evers tribute.

For those unfamiliar with the name, Evers was one of the more outspoken and fervent Black civil rights advocates during this time. A college graduate and decorated soldier, Evers worked tirelessly to end segregation in public schools and elsewhere. He championed economic opportunities and the protection of voting rights for Blacks. Following his appointment as the NAACP's first field secretary for Mississippi in 1954, Evers organized protests, boycotts, and voter registration drives. His efforts and successes over the years made him a target of the KKK and the White Citizens Council, an organization formed to resist integration after the *1954 Brown vs Board of Education* Supreme Court ruling outlawed segregation. He lived under a constant threat of death and often had an FBI escort when he traveled. But for reasons unspecified by the FBI and local police, whose members were rumored to be Klan members, Evers had no such protection as he pulled into his driveway in Jackson after an NAACP meeting just after midnight on June 12, 1963, just hours after JFK's nationally televised civil rights address. As he exited his vehicle and headed toward his house, he was struck in the back by an assassin's bullet. He was rushed to the local hospital but was originally denied entrance because of his race. Eventually, he was allowed to enter – the first Negro admitted to an all-white hospital in Mississippi – but died an hour later, just three weeks before his 38th birthday. The assailant – Byron de la Beckworth – was arrested and charged with murder, but two all-white juries could not reach a guilty verdict, and he was free until 1994, when a third trial, thanks to new evidence, finally resulted in a conviction. Beckworth was sentenced to life in prison and remained incarcerated until his death in 2001.[46]

As the date of Ever's assassination falls squarely between Mr. Sims' last two communiqués, the contrast in tone and content between the two is undeniable and understandable, given Sims' reverence for the man, as evidenced in the poem. The handwritten portion reads as follows: "I hope to have this published and copyrighted in the hope of establishing a fund for the Evers family and the 'Fighting Funds for Freedom.' In my next letter to you folks, I hope I'll be able to send you a real copy, if I'm successful in getting the cooperation of the local branch of the N.A.A.C.P. and a few of my people."

Was the poem copyrighted? Were funds raised for the Evers family? Unknown, as the topic is not discussed in subsequent communication between the families and a scouring of the internet produced no matches under the given title.

---

[46] Medgar Evers. (2024, September 21). In Wikipedia.
https://en.wikipedia.org/wiki/Medgar_Evers

TITLE   "UNSPOKEN SENTIMENTS"
LOVE ONES

I.

As Death summons; as life's journey ends,
Weep not for me, love ones; your broken hearts will mend.

II.

If anyone ask why I chose to stand and fight,
Tell them for democracy and freedom; a word called equal rights.

III.

Feel no anger, love ones; you must not despair,
I leave you my legacy; freedom in the air.

IV.

Trod in my footsteps, love ones; over the ~~perilous~~ perilous path proceed
The assassin silenced my voice; but not my words and deeds.

V.

Freedom is priceless, love ones, guard freedom in trouble and strife
Let no man deny you freedom; let no man deny you life.

VI.

Stand together, love ones; carry on the fight,
Unite for freedom, justice, equality,
that which you know is right

VII.

Pledge to me, love ones; before I go to rest
You will stand up for freedom; In the North, South, East and West.

VIII.

My last request, love ones; before I'm on my way,
Tell America Medgar Evers died for democracy today.

By David Sims

I hope to have this published and copyrighted
in the hope of establishing a fund for the "Evers" Family
and the "Fighting funds for freedom."
In my next letter to you folks I hope I'll be able to
send you a real copy. If I'm successful in getting the cooperation
of the local Branch of the N.A.C.P. and a few of my people

August 14, 1963
314 So. Illinois St.
South Bend 19, Indiana

Dearest friends,

Today, I am heartsick beyond words. A few minutes ago, I ran across your letter of June 23rd and am rereading it. I discovered an inexcusable error on my part in my last letter to you folks. You and Marienus will never realize the pain I feel when I think of my carelessness.

Uppermost in our hearts and minds and always in our daily prayers, we pray for God's mercy and preservation of his children. Needlessly, I say to you folks, we were and shall ever be concerned about the health and welfare of all the people of your area, especially so when an imminent danger exists, such as you described in regards to your Dad's sister. We pray you find it in your hearts to forgive this gross, unpardonable error on my part.

Ruby constantly reminds me of the dangers of trying to "absorb too much of everything and not take time to look at myself." What she really means is that I am so engrossed and concerned about what is happening during this "national crisis" that I lose sight of my most precious concern. She is so right.

Roselyn and Sharkey, please try to understand that with events happening so rapidly and so often to our people and because I am so concerned about the outcome of these events during the past several months, I have found it impossible to put my mind at ease. I can't study properly. I can't even find the time to be concerned about my immediate needs. I find myself wondering, should our people confront yours, if they will be justified in their demands, correct in their approach, and have the type of leadership that will not desert or retreat from their stand if they are fighting for what is right.

In attempting to keep up with what is going on in our area, trying to concentrate on my school work, home life, etc., I feel I have taxed myself too much. In short, I don't know whether I'm coming or going. Realizing that all of my concerns are just too much for anyone, I must make an adjustment.

Actually, at the time I wrote you last, I wrote from faint memories during the time we had and still have somewhat of a crisis here. The appointment of a biracial committee by the mayor includes the selection of Negroes who many of us feel do not know the needs of the Negro masses. In South Bend, they are known as "moderate Negroes"; that is, those professionals who have steady jobs, a decent home, and are pretty comfortable. These people have no desire to irritate white liberals and so-called moderates with actual charges of discrimination, for some of those selected to serve on the committee are the same people who head the unions and corporations who have practiced discrimination against our people for years. You see, our people know that Mr. McMillan, vice-president of

Studebaker Corporation, or Mr. Ladd, president of the Industrial Union Council of St. Gae County, can tell Mr. Brown, of the Urban League, or Dr. Chamblee, that discrimination doesn't exist in the union or the plants, and that anything workers say is just so much baloney. And believe me when I say it is extremely difficult – if not impossible – to prove discrimination exists the way the set-up works. I'll explain it to you folks some time. As things now stand, we "grassroots Negroes" have a tremendous fight on our hands to try to get results.

I realize there is no excuse for my neglect in not taking the time to find your letter and answer the contents, item by item. I've attempted to display what has taken constant precedence over everything else in my overworked mind. Here's hoping and praying you do understand that, ordinarily, I am not this kind of haphazard person at all.

Our deepest, heartfelt sympathy and prayers for strength to all of you during this time. Above all, we pray this letter hasn't arrived too late.

With all our love,

David, Ruby, and children

P.S. It is possible we may see you sometime in September. Also, Dora asked me to explain to you folks that she is a poor writer. But she is a grand person, believe me.

Several noteworthy items here. Having scrutinized David Sims' previous letter, no error could be found so egregious as to elicit such a response. Perhaps it is an error of omission – something he noticed while rereading Mrs. Davids' letter of June 23rd that should have been addressed in his July 13th missive. Might it be related to the "imminent danger" spoken of in the second paragraph? Quite possibly, though, without Roselyn's correspondence, this cannot be verified. Quizzing surviving Davids family members produced no viable clues as to what peril this is a reference to. Roselyn's father, Walter Attig, had several siblings, but by 1963, only two sisters remained: Christine Eggerth and Esther Kruse (a half-sister by Walter's mother's second marriage). The latter passed away in December of 1963, so one might reason that the "danger" was a reference to her failing health.

It seems Mr. Sims is finally coming to the realization that his crusade – however righteous it may be – is negatively impacting his ability to function adequately as a breadwinner, husband, and father. Will he make the necessary "adjustment"? Time will tell.

Finally, both families spoke of visiting each other often. They did not want the 1961 farm visitation to be a one-off. The September visit mentioned in the "P.S." indicates that an effort was still being made by the Sims to get back to the Davids' homestead. Would such a trip come to pass? Mr. Sims addresses this in his next bit of correspondence.

September 26, 1963
314 So. Illinois St.
South Bend, Indiana 46619

Dearest friends,

Today, as our nation prays for atonement, each true heart grieves with pain. It means everything to our people to have friends such as you folks. As you know, our hopes and salvation rest primarily with the hearts and consciences of your people.

The "Birmingham Blasters" are a product of our society who cannot be held responsible for their inhumane crimes against our people. The most vital thing for the American people to understand is the deepened hatred, contempt, and total disregard for our people's lives that exist in this nation today.

244 years of chattel slavery and 100 years of deprivation have cost our people no less than 100 million lives, according to Bertrand Russell, a conservative Englishman. So, you see, the atrocities that school many of your people into shock don't seem to bother others in the least, including many of our own people, who have grown to accept whatever the white man does or says to them as "natural or to be expected". This is the true, extremely dangerous situation that exists in our country today.

Those of you who realize the true picture must not think that these crimes will shock the majority of Americans into a sense of "attitude change", for the vast majority have no desire to see a change come about at this time. Our people are viewed as unwanted, unneeded competitors in this race for life. If given equal opportunity, the Whites feel Negroes will "take their jobs, their homes, and their government", as the ordinary man puts it. Compound this with the fact that the government has forecasted that 22 million jobs will be eliminated within the next decade due to automation, then I am sure you can get a true picture of the white working man's fears. Believe me when I say this situation is a lot more serious than many people realize.

A group of citizens are bringing Dr. King to South Bend on October 18. If weather permits, could you folks plan to be with us? Ruby just returned from the hospital. She had pneumonia; however, due to God's mercy, she is coming along just fine. Prior to receiving your letter, I had written you folks as to why we can't visit you this weekend, as we wanted so desperately to do at this time. Ruby's illness and her recently acquired job dashed all hopes, as this job requires her presence every weekend of the month but one. We still plan and hope to be able to see you folks as soon as possible.

Please forgive my backwardness in this letter. We take it for granted that you all know that we are concerned for your well-being. Extend our love and best wishes. We pray for your success in the "trip to Korea". We are certain God will smile on you for

```
years to come for this action.

Love always,
David & Ruby Sims and family
```

~~~~~~

One cannot help but wonder about the wording of the "Birmingham Blasters" sentence. Perhaps Mr. Sims meant that either the perpetrators wouldn't be held responsible, as no jury in Alabama would convict them, or that their actions are simply an understandable consequence of the hatred and bigotry fomented for generations in this country by those who see Black people as inferior and a threat.

The "Birmingham Blasters"[47] were allegedly members of the Klan and/or the Birmingham police department who, on May 11th, bombed the parsonage of Rev. A. D. King, brother of Martin Luther King Jr., and a nearby motel where King and other African American leaders of the "Birmingham campaign" had been staying. Organized by the Southern Christian Leadership Conference, the movement's members had just the day before negotiated "The Birmingham Truce Agreement" with local officials to desegregate businesses. Promises were also made to advance economic opportunities for African Americans and to release those arrested in recent demonstrations. At that time, Birmingham was considered the most segregated city in America. Demonstrators were met with fire hoses and snarling dogs. The detonation of the bombs lit a powder keg of tension that had been

---

[47] Birmingham riot of 1963. (2024, June 1). In Wikipedia. https://en.wikipedia.org/wiki/Birmingham_riot_of_1963

building for weeks, and peaceful marches turned into riots. News of the unrest quickly reached President Kennedy, who, after learning Governor George Wallace had withdrawn state troopers, deployed federal soldiers to quell the violence. It marked the first time in modern history that the U.S. government deployed military power in response to civil unrest without a specific legal injunction to enforce. This event influenced Kennedy to propose the aforementioned civil rights bill, which was eventually signed into law by Kennedy's successor, Lyndon Johnson. The incident was, sadly, also a harbinger of things to come.

So, plans for the long-awaited Sumner Center sequel were dashed by Ruby's bout with pneumonia, coupled with the mandatory weekend hours of the job she secured. While the latter put a crimp on their travel plans, it was undoubtedly a welcome addition to the family income. An alternative was proposed: the families – or at least the adults – could instead meet up in South Bend in October as Martin Luther King Jr. was to be in town on the 18th, an opportunity Roselyn and Sharkey would surely savor. But could they swing it with the Korea trip looming in November?

~~~~~~

November 10, 1963
314 South Illinois Street
South Bend, Indiana 46619

Dear friends,

We received your letter. As always, we were happy to hear from you. We pray for your good health and spirit, as well as the area's residents. You folks can rest assured as you travel across the world to salvage two precious lives, our community prayers travel with you. We know you are faced with many moments of anxiety as to the outcome of your desire to aid these defenseless children. Your efforts and concern warm our hearts, and we are convinced you will be successful, for this is indeed God's will. Ruby mentioned what we all know: a better home for these children couldn't be found anywhere.

During Dr. King's visit to our area, he mentioned India's millions that slept in the streets in Bombay and Calcutta and, in so many words, stated every child of God must be gravely concerned about mankind's plight.

Our rally for the Southern Christian Leadership Conference was a success. $8,000 was raised for our people's struggle for freedom in the South. The center overflowed with people, adults and youth, Black and White. In summation, everything turned out wonderfully. In addition to this rally, another organization has been born in our city known as the "United Negro Council." This is the organization that will shape the future destiny of the Negro and the city of South Bend for generations to come. Pray for our righteousness, Godly humility, and success. We have the mechanics; if only they can be channeled in the proper directions, our city, the nation, and the world will benefit from our actions.

Everyone sends their love and best wishes for your success. The children send a special "hello" to all

```
the littler Davids: Joyce, Greg, and Patricia. We'd
like to hear from you at your convenience.

Love,
Ruby & David Sims and family
```

~~~~~~

It would seem the assembly hosting Martin Luther King Jr. was a rousing success, both in terms of the money raised and the local organization it spawned that Mr. Sims feels will equitably represent the Negro population in his fair city. Roselyn and Sharkey undoubtedly lament not being able to make the trek to South Bend for this event. Given all of the costs and preparations related to the impending trip to Korea, the tenderhearted twosome probably felt one more out-of-state odyssey would stretch them too thin.

The particulars of the Korean adventure, including the trip itself and everything that led up to it, are fascinating enough to be fodder for a separate book (which may get written at some point), but as the reader is likely curious about this incredible excursion, some details will be provided.

The Davids first attempted to adopt a Native American child, but it was for naught due to all the restrictions and red tape. Then, they discovered from friends that an orphanage run by the Holt Agency in South Korea was actively seeking parents who were willing to adopt non-white children living outside of the United States. The catch? Minnesota law required the adopting parents to meet the adoptees in person before the process could begin. That meant going to Korea. Long story short, the Davids, along with 54 other couples from eleven states, chartered a cargo plane to travel from California to Korea and back. Roselyn and Sharkey had already selected two children from the information provided by the agency. But any adoption procedure is bound to have snafus aplenty, and the Davids' dream of adding two more children to their family was anything but a done deal.

The first setback – and it was a doozy – occurred on November 22. The Davids had already made it to the Golden State, staying with relatives. They boarded the Flying Tiger (likely a C-46 or CL-44) along with the other couples. Mind you, this was not a passenger plane, so comfort was in short supply. Just as the plane was preparing for take-off, the pilots got the horrifying news: President Kennedy had been shot, and everything was on lockdown. Anxious passengers waited and prayed for the best, but it was not to be. JFK's assassination sent shockwaves throughout the nation, and all flights, including those leaving the contiguous states, were delayed or cancelled. Because of the nature of this flight, crew and passengers were able to depart Los Angeles the next day, though the plane was rerouted to Alaska, as stopping in Hawaii was no longer an option (no specifics available as to why). After arriving in Seoul, the prospective parents were taken to the orphanage. The conditions there were deplorable. Most of the children were malnourished; many had diseases and/or deformities. Jonathan, thought to be five years old, had a bum leg, the result of a bout with polio. Maureen, not quite three, was so bloated and weak that the agency suggested the Davids pick a different child, as she wasn't expected to live much longer. But Roselyn, her faith unshaken, responded, "If she dies, she will at least be surrounded by those who love her, and we will have a child in heaven." Roselyn's trust in God's plan was yet again rewarded, and Jonathan and Maureen, along with 85 other Korean orphans, traveled to America with their new adoptive parents. Stories abound regarding how the recent additions to the Davids family regained their health and flourished as they adapted to life on a farm in southern Minnesota but suffice it to say, that's a book for another day.

Chapter 21: Winding Down

The November 10th communiqué would be the last of its kind from either family for 1963. The once-regular letter exchange continued to dwindle to the point where only eight more pieces of correspondence would be mailed: Mr. Sims penned three more missives in 1964 and one in 1965; David III, who joined the Marines after graduating high school, wrote to Roselyn and Sharkey twice in 1966 from the military base in San Francisco where he was stationed; and Ruby sent letters to the Davids in 1971 and again in 1977. Of course, there could have been others, and most likely were, as the verbiage in the 1965 letter seems to indicate.

That said, the decision was made not to reprint the aforementioned letters in their entirety here for a number of reasons. The main purpose of this book is to relate an amazing, uplifting story of two families who forged a unique friendship based on mutual admiration and respect that transcended race and persisted despite numerous hardships. That tale has been told mainly through the correspondence between two incredible individuals. To continue this scintillating saga without the wit and wisdom of one would be an injustice to the reader now that the major events that shaped this captivating kinship have played out.

Another reason for using excerpts going forward is that the four latest missives penned by Mr. Sims, much like the one from July 13th, are dark and, in parts, disturbing, as the charismatic crusader struggles with his faith, finances, and frustration resulting from the indifference so many Americans seem to exhibit toward the plight of

271

his people. The following snippets illustrate the internal and external strife plaguing this troubled titan but also highlight his warmth, understanding, and commitment.

From his letter dated February 16, 1964:

"Yes, God works in mysterious ways. We know our hearts tell us these two children couldn't be located in a better home in America. They will receive an abundance of love, security, Christian fellowship, and understanding, outstanding qualities that radiate from you and Marienus. These qualities, just to mention a few, are those that attract so much of our love for you folks."

"Needlessly, I tell you my indebtedness to your parents and my inability to repay has grievously distressed me more than any single thing during these past years. However, I am happy to say with God's aid by the end of 1964, we hope and pray and shall work hard under extreme difficulties to repay this loan."

"I must confess to you folks I am so disgusted and justifiably angry with the Negro ministry in our city until I have somewhat disassociated myself from the church. The minister in our city has been of the kind Dr. King described as being the taillight rather than the headlight in our struggle for freedom. If there is anything I can't stand, it is a Negro minister who earns his living entirely from goodwill offerings from our people's meager earnings – who will not stand up and be counted on issues of life or death as far as we are concerned. As for me, I sincerely feel until such time a preacher is committed and concerned about the welfare of his community, then I have no desire to be associated with this type of minister."

Mr. Sims also relates that he is still in the M.D.T.A. program and feels that the training he is receiving will help him find meaningful employment, with or without a certificate of completion. Ruby has secured a job at the Holy Cross House, an assisted living facility, on the Notre Dame campus and even David III and Harold have part-time work, yet their combined incomes barely keep them afloat financially.

From his letter dated May 24, 1964:

"This is the third letter I have begun to write since we last heard from you folks. We know your life and love have been enriched by the newest additions to the Davids family. You have so much love in your heart until it radiates and draws others to you. This is a virtue many people do not have and wish they could acquire... Yes, through your letter to us, we share deeply the feeling of joy and a sense of accomplishment. We'll never know the effects upon the lives of others our simple extended hand of friendship has had in restoring man's faith in man."

"I'm exceedingly happy to say I'm again working. As you know, on April 2nd, we completed our training in M.D.T.A. Even though I am not working in the capacity for which I was trained, I am working, and this is something to be thankful for. I commute 17 miles one way daily to work at Clark's Equipment Company, located in Buchanan, Michigan... For the first time since 1959, I feel I have a job upon which I can depend for steady employment at least nine months out of the year. This company supplies General Motors, Ford, and Chrysler Corp. with rear ends for trucks."

"As usual, I am grieved to the depths of my soul since I haven't been able for the past four years to meet my indebtedness to you folks. One can't begin to realize the agony, the pain of despair, the feeling of complete helplessness when one is without a source of income adequate to take care of personal obligations. Roselyn, you and Marienus will never know how much I appreciate your faith, your patience, your forbearance, and long extended confidence you have shown me. When I think maybe this loan has brought an undue hardship to you and your folks, believe me, I die a thousand deaths each day. I'm certain you know this is the last thing in the world I'd want to happen to such wonderful people as you... Life is so uncertain for industrial workers that I dare not again say when or how I will begin repayments on the loan. However, if God sees fit to continue to be merciful to us, I assure each of you someway, someday, somehow, I shall be able to keep my word. This is a solemn vow."

From the letter dated July 14, 1964:

"We have received many blessings since we last met. Ruby's faith has been regenerated. She has been born in the "Church of God in Christ." Today, she stands out as the spiritual leader of this family; for this, I am very thankful. It is my greatest desire to walk with her in righteousness. However, my limited understanding in regards to "today's events and the role of the church" as I see it prohibits me from giving of myself to even consider association with people who profess to be followers of Christ during our lifetime. We see him nailed to the cross in Mississippi, Alabama, and elsewhere, and we never say a mumbling word. I'm often reminded of the time Jesus asked his followers to watch with him one hour while he prayed. Some were weary and fell asleep during this critical hour when their awakeness was requested and most needed by the Master. To me, this is what is happening in our country today. Many professed followers of Christ are weary and asleep when they should be awake... If the millions in this nation who belong to the Christian faith were of Christ and in Christ, would their souls not be troubled? Wouldn't they cry out in a loud voice of anguish? Heaven knows it is not my intention to question God's plan, but I am anxious to see righteousness prevail... If I am correct in my thinking, pray God gives me more strength and understanding to face this crucial test, for indeed, during these perilous times, my soul is deeply troubled. One thing is for sure - I want to be on the side of good and righteousness... I cannot accept that this (poverty, starvation, etc.) is God's plan and that we are not to exert any effort to overcome this situation... I'm willing to give my all to the struggle between good and evil. However, the forces that represent goodness must somehow find a way to let their light so shine that other men may see their good works and desire to gain focus so that righteousness may prevail."

Mr. Sims also asks "exactly when we can expect you and whether or not you will be able to spend the night so we can prepare for you. We are so glad to have you visit us again." Apparently, the Sims are anticipating a visit from the Davids (including Grandma Hunter, whom everyone, especially Freda, is anxious to see) very soon. Whether or not this visit actually took place could not be ascertained. The surviving Sims siblings have no recollection of it, nor is there confirmation in future correspondence. Hence, the last social visit between the two families may very well have taken place at South Bend in April of '63. Sad to say, despite their best efforts and intentions, the Sims never returned to the Sumner Center acreage that, for them, held so many precious memories.

David Sims' final epistle is but two pages on 7×8.5-inch stationery and can best be encapsulated as a plea for prayers for his two eldest. The surviving siblings describe the matters as personal and prefer details not be shared, so their wishes have been honored.

Each of the two letters sent by David III to Roselyn and Sharkey is a hodgepodge of belated birthday wishes for various individuals, greetings to those he met while visiting the farm, inquiries as to the health and well-being of Davids' family members and friends, and, of course, talk of the weather. One specific item worthy of mention is that David III is married and has a child whom he has yet to see. In the letter dated April '66, the proud papa expresses his enthusiasm regarding meeting his at-the-time four-month-old little girl for the first time once he returns home from Camp Pendleton in September. Her name? Rosalind Renee Sims! Obviously, David III holds his "aunt and uncle" in very high esteem.

The feeling is undoubtedly mutual as David III would go on to make them, his family, and everyone who knew him very proud. His unit, much to his mother's chagrin, was deployed to Vietnam not once but twice, where he served honorably. He quickly earned his Private First-Class stripes, unheard of at the time for a Black man. He eventually ascended to the rank of Sergeant and saw extensive combat. Awards included one for marksmanship, as well as the distinguished Purple Heart for being wounded in action. Mr. and Mrs. Sims lobbied for their son to be discharged, and, thanks, in part, to the efforts of their Congressman, David III returned home soon thereafter. The experience left the intrepid soldier scarred emotionally, and to this day, he prefers not to talk about that life-altering experience. What few stories he did share with his parents and siblings were horrors no person should ever have to go through and affirms the well-known adage "war is hell."

277

Ruby's writings consisted of the standard fare from one mother to another: family news. Six years have passed since the last missive from either Sims parent, so "they grow up so fast" comes to mind as Ruby explained the goings-on of her nine children. By 1971, David III and Harold were already married with children. Charlotte had found employment as a telephone operator, Carla Diane and Cheryl were both in college, and Paul worked at a government factory. Only Freda (a senior), Avard (junior high), and Belinda (sixth grade) remained at home. Ruby also expressed how much she misses her Minnesota friends and implored Roselyn to write back and send pictures of her children, who now range in age from nine to fifteen. Sadly, another six years would pass until the next letter, but its contents revealed an unexpected meeting between some members of the two families, albeit under unfortunate circumstances.

The last piece of correspondence between the Sims and Davids is dated 12-19-1977. In it, Ruby speaks of a mysterious auto-immune illness afflicting Belinda, one that required testing by multiple doctors and a longer-than-expected stay before returning home. But home from where? As the letter does not specify, Belinda herself and Patricia Davids Shoemaker (then 15) were relied upon to fill in the blanks. Evidently, Ruby apprised Roselyn of the situation with her youngest daughter (now a senior) and that the Mayo Clinic had been recommended as the best bet to diagnose Belinda's ailment. Having decided upon that course of action, Ruby wanted to know if any of the Davids could meet them at the facility. Of course, Roselyn jumped at the chance to see her dear friend again, and Maureen and Patricia (the only Davids children still at home) were also excited to partake, as the former was not yet a part of the Davids family as of the last Sims-Davids encounter, and the latter was too young to remember. So, in early December (the exact date is unclear), Roselyn, Sharkey, Maureen, and Patricia motored to Rochester to rendezvous with Ruby, David, and Belinda at a restaurant near the clinic. One can only imagine the excitement members of both families must have felt as they laid eyes on one another for the first time in 14 years! For Patricia and Belinda, it must have felt like the first time, and for Maureen, it was. Though neither Belinda nor Patricia remembers the nature of the conversations, safe to say, they likely included plenty of stories involving the exploits of the children, though most were already adults. Belinda's memories of the event are more impressions than specific words or images. She recalls the feeling of exuberance in meeting and interacting with the Davids girls, now teenagers like herself, and that they shared that enthusiasm in getting to know her. But her strongest sense from the occasion was the genuine warmth and love displayed by Roselyn and her mother toward each other. This deep affection permeated the booth where they sat, putting everyone at ease and making the event that much more special.

While a definitive diagnosis was never mentioned (nor confirmed by Belinda), Ruby spoke in the letter of a return visit to the clinic for a second round of tests and treatments scheduled for March of '78 and hoped for the opportunity to see Roselyn and company once again. Belinda verified that this second visit to the Mayo Clinic did indeed occur, but it was just her and her mother, and they did not meet any Davids family members while there. Thus, it can be safely gleaned that the last in-person get-together between any Sims and Davids family members took place at an eatery near the Mayo Clinic in Rochester, Minnesota, in December of 1977, bringing one chapter of their incredible camaraderie to a close.

Chapter 22: Final Thoughts

It is this author's sincere hope that the reader was entertained, educated, and inspired by the contents of this book. While segregation and discrimination have been, for the most part, scoured from the laws and policies of this great nation, the same cannot be said for the hearts of many of its citizens. Vigilance is required on the part of lawmakers and civilians alike to ensure that such statutes are carried out in a way that is fair and just to all Americans, regardless of creed or color. While racism may never be totally eradicated, the Sims and Davids have demonstrated that it need not interfere with the bond that can be forged between peoples when they set aside their differences and understand that we are all children of God, equal in His sight. Quite simply, their unique fellowship was a story that needed to be told.

One other item of note that the reader may be wondering about: Was Mr. Sims finally able to pay back the loan in full and, thus, ease his troubled conscience? As there is no definitive answer in the correspondence and neither set of parents discussed financial matters with their children, one can only speculate. That said, Joyce and Patricia surmise, based on cryptic conversations with their mother as adults, that Mr. Sims paid whatever he could whenever he could but that a balance remained and, at some point, in an act of Christian love and understanding, that amount was simply forgiven.

In sorting through the correspondence and newspaper clippings of Mrs. Davids' scrapbook, something curious was discovered: two pieces of printer paper, upon which was typed a fascinating but incomplete story. Obviously typed on a computer, it was quite out of place with the other relics from the past. But who wrote this, and where is the rest of the story? After a bit of detective work and conversations with Charlotte and Carla Diane, it was deduced that the author was Fredonya's son, Warren, Jr., now a preacher at a church in Cincinnati, Ohio.

Phone numbers were exchanged, and after a wonderful conversation with Mr. Curry, the mystery was unraveled. It turns out that this was a Facebook post meant to pay homage to his mother, Fredonya, who passed away in November of 2016. No further elaboration is necessary as the tribute appears below and is a fitting ending to this tantalizing tale of an indomitable, interracial friendship. The only remaining conundrum? Who printed it out and placed it in Roselyn's scrapbook? While Joyce would be the logical guess, her tech skills, or lack thereof, make this scenario unlikely, plus she made no mention of this before her passing. As such, this puzzling whodunnit will likely remain an intriguing yet irrelevant enigma.

~~~~~~ *GENERATIONAL CALLINGS & BLESSINGS* ~~~~~~

On the morning of March 1, 2006, I had a visitation from the Lord. In this dream, the Lord told me to move my family from my hometown of Milwaukee, WI to Cincinnati, OH to start a new church.

When I asked the Lord why Cincinnati? One of His responses to me was "What are you going to do about the racism down there?" I had no idea what He was talking about. It was only after much prayer and research that I became aware of the racial tensions in this city that I now call home. It became very evident to me at that moment that the Lord was preparing to use my life to tear down racial barriers between Blacks and Whites. It has become part of my life's work.

Recently, as I was thumbing through my mother's belongings after her passing, I came across a paper that she had written for one of her college classes. In this paper, she kept referencing the Summer of 1961 (she was 7 years old) and how that was the best summer of her life. She stated that our family (my grandparents, uncles, and aunts who were all children at the time) were invited to stay with an all-white family in the town of Spring Valley, MN.

This might not seem like a big deal now but the fact of the matter is, this was a very dangerous thing back in the early 60's. Frolicking and building relationships with Whites for Blacks could have literally cost you your life. This was during the height of segregation, Jim Crow, etc. in the U.S.

Anyways, I came to find out that a white family invited my grandparents and their children to stay with them for a week in their home in Spring Valley, MN. Whites in Spring Valley had never seen what they called "Negroes" (Black Americans) in person. Some were excited about the Davids family (this is the white family in MN) inviting the Sims family to visit them, but many Whites were not happy about this. They did not want Negroes invading this all-white community. After much time and deliberation, my grandparents accepted the invitation and went to go and stay with this family. Their obedience in this matter was the beginning of breaking down racial hostilities between Blacks and Whites.

Their story caught the attention over at Jet Magazine. It was so fascinating, what these two families were doing, that Jet decided to write an entire piece on their story.

Fast forward....so after coming across this info after reading my mom's paper, I said to myself "I wonder if Jet archived their publications? If so, I wonder can I find the story that my mom made mention of in her writings?"

It took me a few hours to comb through the online archives of Jet's publications, but after doing some digging, I found it. I found the piece that Jet wrote on my family being involved in an interracial experiment to tear down racial walls. I was literally in tears when I found this piece. Why?

Because it helped to add some context to the passions of my life and beat of my heart. Why have I always been so passionate about Blacks and Whites coming together? Was this something that I was just innately born with? Possibly, but now I know that it was (and still is) a part of a generational calling upon my family.

Know that for many of you, the baton has been handed down to you through generations. What you have been called to finish, someone else in your family may have been called to start. Do not take lightly the work that you are currently doing.

Find purpose in your passion and walk with God to impact the lives of those whom He has placed in your care.

I hope that you all enjoy reading through this article as much as I did. It was pretty cool to see a picture of my mom, Freda Curry, at 7 years old, riding on the back of a cow with her brother Paul Dagood Guy, who was 10 years old at the time.

I am thankful to the Lord that even in death, good things arise out of the ashes.

The End

Acknowledgements

As a fitting conclusion, those who made the telling of this awe-inspiring odyssey possible must be acknowledged. Naming names is precarious, lest someone be left out, but is necessary nonetheless.

A very special thank-you to the surviving members of the Sims family: David III, Paul, Cheryl, Charlotte, Carla Diane, and Belinda. Without permission to use their father's letters, this book would not have been possible. The latter three provided remembrances of their experiences with the Davids, further enhancing the impact of the story. It was truly an honor to become acquainted with such exemplary people.

Likewise, a note of appreciation to Greg Davids and Maureen Davids Grimaud for allowing the use of their mother's missives, but special kudos to Patricia "Patty" Davids Shoemaker. She wore many hats: emotional support, sounding board, editor. With Joyce's passing, this author often needed someone to bounce ideas off of, share successes with, or just chat about the mundane things of life. Pat became that someone.

Gratitude must also be extended to Warren Curry, Jr. for providing that exemplary tribute to his mother, Fredonya. Curry extols each of us to "find purpose in your passion," a credo exemplified by the audacious authors who penned the correspondence that fueled this needful narrative.

A huge shout-out to all the magazines and newspapers whose articles provided the facts and perspectives necessary for the reader to truly grasp the enormity of the events which took place. The works of these estimable establishments are cited in the footnotes but special mention must be made of David Pennington, author of many of the Rochester Post-Bulletin articles. His insightful etchings added much detail to the account of that wondrous week at the Davids' farm in the summer of '61 that would otherwise be missing.

It goes without saying that the allure of this tantalizing tale would be noticeably lessened without the letters from Peter Lassally, the producer of Image Series. He cared enough to see to it that Mrs. Davids' first letter got into the right hands and corresponded with her and with Mr. Sims to help facilitate their budding friendship. The utilization of these letters required his permission, and when that was not possible due to his failing health, his son, Tom, stepped up and, after reviewing said letters, graciously granted permission for their usage here.

And lastly, a tip of the hat to Hemingway Publishers for their proofreading, editing, formatting, and cover design services. Many other publishers offered to produce this book, but Hemingway provided the best combination of features, price, and service.